Dear Chad
Thank you so much for
faithfully Preaching The Word.
I have given this Book To
A Couple of Pastor's That I

OUTHOUSE ADVENTURES

SHORT STORIES FOR SPORTSMEN ON THE GO!

have Sat under And Mean
A lot To us. May God Bless
you And Karen with Many
More faithful years of Service.
In Christ's Service
Tom Schubring

TOM SCHUBRING

WESTBOW
PRESS®
A DIVISION OF THOMAS NELSON
& ZONDERVAN

WestBow Press books may be ordered through booksellers or by contacting:

WestBow Press
A Division of Thomas Nelson & Zondervan
1663 Liberty Drive
Bloomington, IN 47403
www.westbowpress.com
1 (866) 928-1240

Interior Image Credit: Anita Schubring

Scripture quotations taken from the New American Standard Bible® (NASB), Copyright © 1960, 1962, 1963, 1968, 1971, 1972, 1973, 1975, 1977, 1995 by The Lockman Foundation Used by permission. www.Lockman.org

ISBN: 978-1-9736-6948-7 (sc)
ISBN: 978-1-9736-6949-4 (hc)
ISBN: 978-1-9736-6947-0 (e)

Library of Congress Control Number: 2019909822

Print information available on the last page.

WestBow Press rev. date: 8/6/2019

FOREWORD

Reading Tom Schubring's Outhouse Adventures made me realize just how much our lives share some common characteristics: our love of the hunt and being mystified and drawn to the amazing flight of an arrow at an early age. We both were hooked! Tom's book is a collection of short stories centering around archery and what it takes to be a good hunter.

Tom writes with passion and talks about setting goals and how practice helps make you a better, ethical hunter. He talks about passing up on an animal in hopes of a bigger one and not shooting the first one that comes along. Tom said it best: "There's no shame in an empty tag."

Tom writes from his heart about the vast experiences he's had and how he enjoys the sights, sounds, and smells of God's great outdoors, and through his book, he makes the reader feel like they are right there with him while on his quest to harvest one of his favorite game animals.

It's a journey in pursuit of his dreams, no matter the circumstances, outcomes, or misadventures. Tom connects the dots by using each story to include his feelings and emotions. He tells of the lessons we can learn from those feelings and emotions. He includes Bible verses and tells us that the love of hunting is similar to our relationship with the Lord.

Ray Howell, March 17, 2019

INTRODUCTION

Many of us know of someone that has experienced an almost unbelievable situation during their time afield. I am that guy. If something weird or out of the norm is going to happen, chances are I'm somehow involved. In over forty years of bow hunting deer, elk, turkeys, and bear, I've had more than my share of misadventures. From grizzly charges to wolf attacks, I think I've experienced it all. This book is a collection of some of those stories. It is in no way intended to be a brag book, as many of these humorous stories focus on what went wrong rather than on what went right. After all, we usually learn a lot more from our mistakes than from our successes.

Why Outhouse Adventures? Well, truth be told, I really don't enjoy reading. It's not the reading part I don't enjoy; it's the sitting still part I dislike. I have found most guys are wired the same way. If you do most of your reading from the comfort of your family bathroom, then this book is for you! Each chapter stands alone and contains some short stories that will entertain and challenge you. So put down the seat, turn on the fan, and hang out the do not disturb sign. Enjoy.

DEDICATION

This book is dedicated to all those who have gone before me. It's for all the men and women who invested in my life and are no longer with us in bodily form—my parents and grandparents, my aunts and uncles, and especially two of my children, the one I never had the privilege to meet and Zak, my firstborn. The memories of the times we spent afield together bring a smile to my face as well as a tear to my eye. I miss you, bud!

I also want to thank my loving wife for putting up with me and all my time afield, as well as allowing all those antlers and fish to decorate our walls. You're the greatest! Above all, I want to thank my Lord and Savior Jesus Christ, who saved me time and time again, not only physically but also spiritually. You truly are King of Kings and Lord of Lords!

ZAK AND ANITA
Zak Schubring, July 8, 1990–January 30, 2018

CONTENTS

CHAPTER 1

Lifetime Pursuit

I grew up reading *Outdoor Life* and *Bowhunter* magazines. The western adventures of Jim Carmichael, Larry D. Jones, Dwight Schuh, M. R. James, Chuck Adams, and many others absolutely fascinated me. I have to admit the main reasons I had for enlisting in the US Air Force were thirty days of paid vacation each year and resident big game tags out west! My dream sheet consisted of bases located in Montana, Wyoming, and Colorado. God graciously answered my prayers by landing me in Colorado Springs.

The adventures I had only previously dreamed about were soon to become a reality! I was in such a hurry to get out west that I celebrated my eighteenth birthday in basic training. Basic training is where I learned invaluable skills, like how to properly fold my socks and underwear. My basic training was followed up by four months of technical training at the Brooks Air Force Base School of Aerospace Medicine in San Antonio, Texas. It wasn't until December 1983 that I finally arrived in Colorado Springs. My late-December arrival prevented me from enjoying that fall's hunt.

I was blessed with two roommates who were bowhunters. They had arrived in Colorado about six months before I had. That meant

Pete and Paul had already accomplished the hard work of finding an area to hunt. Ironically, both of my roommates were country boys from my home state of Wisconsin. And to no surprise, both had enlisted for the same reasons I had: to elk hunt on Uncle Sam! *Did I mention I love this great country?*

The next nine months flew by as we passed our free time practicing with our bows, scouting, camping, or simply wetting a line. We talked and dreamed constantly of opening weekend. With the big weekend approaching, we were naively confident that we would all tag out our first morning.

After a long four-hour drive to South Fork, we finally arrived at camp about nine o'clock Friday night. An hour later, our camp was set up, and we were dreaming of our first elk harvest.

Early the next morning, we hiked in the inky darkness to our predetermined morning ambush spots. The elk were fairly predictable at that time of year: feeding in the aspens and meadows all night long before returning to the dark timber in the morning. We had set up our blinds along their favorite travel routes in the hope of intercepting them. What could possibly be simpler?

The guys and I were all shivering in our chosen locales for a good half hour before shooting light arrived. As I waited in the dark, anticipating the outcome of my first elk hunt, it happened! I could hear the elk starting to travel through. This was not good! It was still too dark to shoot! And instead of traveling down through my valley, they stayed well above me, paralleling my trail as they clung to the ridge. It was still black as coal in the valley, but the elk were clearly visible, sky-lined against the lightening eastern horizon.

I started to count them as they passed by: one, two, three, ten, fifteen, twenty, thirty elk! The herd included several bulls, and one was a real whopper. The biggest bull hesitated on the ridge and let out a hair-raising bugle. His huge whale tails were touching his hams as his bellow echoed up the valley. This was the first bugle I had ever heard. The hair on the back of my neck stood up as shivers ran down my spine.

Everything I had dreamed of was happening. But my lifelong dream was quickly becoming a nightmare as the animals were seventy-five yards away and heading out of my life. I had to do something.

Remembering the elk whistle my first sergeant had given me—and with nothing to lose—I figured it was now or never. (This "whistle," as he called it, consisted of a half-inch-diameter piece of metal conduit with a chunk of wood crammed into one end of it. A little green spray paint was added to cover up its shine.) I'm sure Will Primos would have been impressed.

I put that whistle to my lips and let out a high-pitched squeal. To my delight, a five-by-five satellite bull answered and made his way down the hill to show me who was boss. He stopped in the dark shadows to survey the situation as I waited silently for daylight. He didn't find his challenger, and I could hear him starting to walk away. So I whistled again. I was greeted with an immediate screaming response as he angrily committed to kicking my butt! He charged in, stopping about fifteen yards away. He then proceeded to bugle, grunt, pant, and snort as he destroyed a ten-foot pine tree directly in front of me. I'm sure the snot was flying as he put on his show. But it was still too dark to shoot. All I could see in the darkness was the top of that pine tree whipping like a flagpole in a hurricane.

Growing up milking cows in Wisconsin had accustomed me to the size of large animals. I have even experienced my share of leaping over fences to escape the occasional rogue bull! But most bovines are actually quite docile. This old boy was anything but docile. And if there was a fence to be had, I would have jumped over it. Fences I didn't have but pistols I did. I pulled my sidearm. As I nervously awaited daylight, the wind swirled, and the bull busted me. He sounded like a runaway stagecoach as he trotted off to catch up with the rest of the herd.

When shooting light finally arrived, I continued to blow the whistle, to no avail. After a few hours of blind squealing, I walked over and checked out the damage the bull had done to that innocent little tree. It was thoroughly trashed.

Awesome! This was even more exciting than I ever dreamed it would be. The thrill of my first elk hunt was everything I had hoped for—minus, of course, a shot opportunity. That encounter was also filled with a wide range of emotions, from anticipation and excitement to fears. That included both the fear of missed opportunities as well as fear for my life!

Later that morning when I met up with the guys, I was still incredibly pumped up. Ironically, I was still holding onto my pistol. We all got a big laugh out of my first up-close elk encounter. I caught flack for years for pulling my pistol that morning. But good-natured ribbing is all part of the experience. That encounter left me more determined than ever to harvest one of those magnificent animals with my bow. And for the record, I never again felt compelled to draw my pistol or jump a fence!

I was not only drawn to elk, but I had become a fully addicted elkaholic! The idea of calling elk became my passion. For the next twelve months, I could be found reading everything I could find on calling elk. I purchased cassette tapes by Larry D. Jones. My constant practicing drove my entire dorm floor nuts as bugles echoed down the halls.

I learned to use a diaphragm call. I practiced mimicking all of Larry's calls until I could no longer feel my tongue. I had totally memorized his tapes and still laugh at him explaining that the "popping sound you hear is the rain hitting the microphone." I guess you had to be there.

So was all my practice worth it? Absolutely! Through a lot of trial and error, I have had countless awesome experiences. I've been blessed with having hundreds of deer, elk, bear, wolves, coyotes, and turkeys respond to my calls. Many of these critters hang on my walls, while many more are displayed on my friends' walls. When I think back on all my adventures, having started with a borrowed piece of conduit and a dream, I can only shake my head.

Hard work and God's faithfulness have taken me a long way. God's faithfulness was evident as I look back on my life's pursuit of him also. From my rough teenage years to my time in the service,

God never stopped pursuing me. I was in my twenties when I finally stopped running away from God. Along with my new bride, we dedicated our lives to him. The more we pursued him, the more evident his love and concern for us became.

After thirteen years working in maintenance and engineering, I left the factory for a missionary position in a large Christian camp. There I had the privilege to teach hundreds of kids to shoot bows and hundreds more about outdoor education. I had the privilege to speak on many adventure trips, such as rock climbing, kayaking, canoeing, and backpacking trips. I was pursuing God, and he was giving me the desires of my heart. I was blessed with the opportunity to do exactly what I loved to do.

Although I often didn't have two nickels to rub together, God was working out the details for western hunts better than I could've ever imagined. I eventually answered the call to pastor a church in southern Wisconsin. God continued to open doors as I've been privileged to publicly share my passion for hunting, calling, and Jesus around the Midwest as I've spoken at different camps, game feeds, and churches. Although I still don't have two nickels to rub together, I couldn't imagine a better life.

> Trust in the Lord and do good; Dwell in the land and cultivate faithfulness. Delight yourself in the Lord; And He will give you the desires of your heart. Commit your way to the Lord, Trust also in him and He will do it. (Psalm 37:3–5 NASB)

I have pursued a relationship with God and his Son, Jesus. In other words, I have "delighted myself in the Lord." And he has given me the desires of my heart.

Have you? What are you pursuing that's leaving you empty and unfulfilled? Try delighting yourself in Jesus today. Focus on what he has done for you, and you'll be amazed at how your life will change for the better.

CHAPTER 2

A Bad Day

Opening weekend of bow season was hot and humid. It was the middle of September 2003, and despite the warm weather, we were going hunting. During the previous spring, I had found several nice shed antlers while scouting this property. Mid-eighties or not, something needed to go down!

My first opportunity to hunt came on Sunday afternoon. Tony and I drove alongside the farm to the edge of the eighty we were planning to hunt. The land was a mixture of select cut, swamp, and poplar slashing. The slashing was a thick stand of two-inch-diameter poplar trees. The east side of the property bordered a dairy farm, while the swampy west side continued on for over fifteen miles before it crossed the first road. This was big north woods country!

Our plan was to set up about fifty yards apart, just off an alfalfa field with our climbing tree stands. I wasn't going to let anything get me down that day, not even the radio announcers' play-by-play of my beloved Packers getting destroyed by the Colts.

I had built my climbing tree stand as a high school shop project and was still using it twenty-five years later. For the record, that's not a good idea! I wrapped the angled iron V around the tree, tightened the wing nuts, stuffed my toes under the fan belt, and up the tree I went ... sort of. If you've never used or seen one of these baker-style stands, you're in for a treat!

You must first reach as high as you can and bearhug the tree. Then you tilt the stand down with your toes and pull the stand up with your stomach and leg muscles. Then tilt the stand back to the level position, stand up, and repeat the process. You ascend or descend the tree about six inches at a time. If you hunt a lot, by the end of bow season, you're guaranteed to be rocking six-pack abs.

The tree I chose was a good-sized poplar. These trees have very smooth bark but also have sporadic rough patches. My ascent was when my problems really began. The stand was not gripping the tree properly, and every time I went up three feet, I would slide back down two and a half feet. My bare arms were getting ripped to shreds by the rough patches of bark. What would normally have taken me five minutes to go up twenty feet had taken me over twenty minutes.

When I finally did make it to my destination, I was dripping with sweat and blood and totally exhausted! Then when I pulled my compound bow up the tree, it got caught on a branch. As I worked to free it, my cable popped off of the cams! If you're not familiar with compound bows, in layman's terms, I broke my bow. Badly!

Optimistic by nature, I was only temporarily defeated. I descended the tree and gathered my gear. After telling Tony my saga, I headed back to the truck, not wanting to jeopardize his hunt. I had informed him that if I could fix my bow, I would just finish out my hunt closer to the truck.

First things first. I checked the score of the game and was pleasantly surprised that the Pack had scored twice! Cool! Now they were only down by twenty-four points. Things were looking up! I attached a ratchet strap to my cams and used it to compress my bow limbs, which allowed me to get the cables back on. But in the process, I knelt in a thorn bush and spent the next fifteen minutes pulling spines out of my leg.

But on the bright side, my bow was operational! I decided to take a test shot, just to reassure myself everything was working correctly. After picking out a leaf on a distant dirt bank, I squeezed the trigger on my release. I watched as my arrow sliced through the air and hit its mark. Crack! Hmmmm, it seemed there was a large rock behind the leaf, which shattered my arrow.

Always an eternal optimist, I was elated that my bow worked! I grabbed my gear and set up about 150 yards west of the truck. I located a heavy game trail about thirty yards off the poplar slashing. This time I wisely chose to climb a big maple in a relatively open select cut. Five minutes later, I was settled in for the evening hunt. I thought to myself, This just may work after all! I still had two hours to hunt until dark.

About an hour later, two does worked their way out of the slashing. Wisconsin had an "earn a buck" regulation at the time, which meant that I had to harvest a doe before I could legally shoot a buck. I'm personally all in favor of harvesting excess does. It's a good management practice, besides the fact that they are delicious. But I was convinced at the time that "earn a buck" was some type of communist plot to ruin America!

The lead doe was feeding broadside at thirty yards. I patiently waited for both of their heads to go down, and then I drew my bow back and took careful aim. My release seemed perfect, but the does went all parkour on me and vacated the area before my arrow even got there. Dumbfounded, I couldn't understand why she was so wired on opening weekend.

I only had to wait about twenty minutes to receive the answer to my question. A lone, eerie howl erupted from the slashing below me. It was followed by a chorus of howls sung by the rest of the pack. Wolves! Great! Just what this night needed! It was time to put a fork in it because this hunt was done.

As legal shooting hours neared their end, I climbed down to look for my arrow, with no success. I returned to my tree to retrieve my stand and a headlamp. It was twilight—still light enough to see but yet gray enough that a light might help me find the arrow.

As I searched the grass and leaves for the arrow, the woods around me erupted with wolves! The entire pack burst out of the slashing and surrounded me. The nearest wolf was only about eight feet away. He was big and black, and his eyes glowed an eerie Halloween orange in my headlamp. Wolves were on either side of and behind me! Several were within only a few yards, while others circled at a distance. Although I didn't count, I later found out there were eleven wolves in that pack.

I raised my bow above my head to look as big as 160-pound redneck can look and hollered at them. I proceeded to knock an arrow. I figured if I was going down, it wouldn't be alone! I stamped my feet at them, all the while yelling, "Get out of here! Go on, beat it!"

They just stared at me and circled. I believe they were contemplating what I was and how I would taste. As I slowly backed toward the truck, I hollered, "Tony!"

"Yah!" was his reply.

"Get over here!" I yelled.

Vroooom! I was both surprised and elated to hear my old truck start up. Seeing Tony bouncing down that logging road was really a sight for sore eyes! As Tony neared, the wolves retreated back into the poplar slashing.

"Whew! That was close," I said to Tony. Then I asked him, "Just what were you doing back at the truck so early? Did you get a deer?"

Tony replied, "As soon as you left, a pack of wolves showed up! Not wanting to walk back in the dark, as soon as they left, I left! I had no idea where you were, so I just sat in the truck and waited for you."

It would be safe to say that most of you will never experience a wolf encounter like I had. But we have all had bad days—days' when we just want to give up and sit in the truck. Or worse, days' when we try to run away from our fears and problems! I am certain if I had tried to run away, I would not be here today. I would have been considered prey and an easy meal for the wolves. A couple of wolves can easily take down a thousand-pound moose. A loud, skinny redneck wouldn't even be considered sport to them.

The Bible calls the devil our enemy, our adversary, the father of all lies, murder, and thief.

Be of sober spirit, your adversary, the devil, prowls around like a roaring lion, seeking someone to devour. But resist him, firm in your faith, knowing that the same experiences of suffering are being accomplished by your brethren who are in the world. (1 Peter 5:8–9)

Like the wolves, the devil feeds off of fear and vulnerability. He likes to blindside us when we are either doing great and not expecting it or when we are sick of fighting and ready to give up! It's in those times, when your circumstances have you worn down, that you must really determine in your heart to stand firm and not give up.

Submit to God, resist the devil and he will flee from you! Just as the wolves did. I stood my ground and called for back up. God is our back up and when we submit to him the Devil flees. (James 4:7)

CHAPTER 3

Fearful to Fearless

Most people suffer from some sort of fear or anxiety. It could be snakes, spiders, bears, heights, or maybe even your mother-in-law. Maybe it's the fear of losing a loved one or your employment. The list is endless. It's interesting that public speaking closely follows death as the top two fears in all of America. Ridiculous, isn't it? Yes, but aren't all fears? Would you like to know how to turn your flight instincts into fight instincts? Well, listen up, guys, because screaming like a little girl when you see a spider will get your man card revoked, and no one wants that!

My youngest son, Mark, works as a big game guide in Wyoming. His stories of fearless adventures in grizzly country have always captivated me. He recently sent me pictures of a sleeping grizzly he had taken with his cell phone. No big deal, right? At the time he was alone thirty miles from the trailhead, leading a pack string of horses and mules loaded down with fresh elk meat. He has had many close calls and encounters over the years, and I can't help but remember back to when this now-fearless young man was a scared little boy. There were several notable aha moments during his maturing process.

In the previous chapter, I shared my encounter with the wolf pack. Well, the story didn't end there. The very next day, I was bowhunting again. This time, I was hunting in some mature hardwoods about thirty miles southeast of my wolf encounter.

The day was perfect, seventy degrees, sunny, and calm. My stand was high atop an oak ridge. My oldest son, Zak, was sitting about 150 yards north of me on the intersection of some game trails. The largest trail crossed a creek, or crick, as we call them up north. About an hour after we had set up, I heard what sounded like a car door slam. I knew instantly it was Zak's ancient compound bow. If silence is golden, his bow rates' cast iron!

As I pondered the possible outcome of his shot, he came running up the trail to me. He was hollering, "I just shot a buck! I just shot a buck!" I still wonder today if he didn't make it down the tree before his arrow had hit the deer.

Zak had just shot his first deer with a bow! The deer was a world record fork horn. Zak was thirteen at the time, and his excitement was uncontainable! Mine either, for that matter! After a quick discussion, we proceeded to drive the five miles home to give the deer time to expire just in case it hadn't already.

Zak was a very quiet boy by nature, but he chattered like a squirrel all the way home! After checking in with Mom, we gathered the lanterns and of course got Mark. Mark was nine at the time, and he had been on almost every family tracking job since he was three years old. Mark's job was to stand by the last blood with his little lantern as we circled out farther and farther looking for the next drops of blood.

This particular blood trail went from great to nonexistent. As we widened our search, Mark was left alone in the dark. Keep in mind this was only twenty-four hours after dear old dad had his wolf encounter. The stage had been set! With his little mind racing wildly we heard, "Hey! Where are you guys? Where you guys at? Stop going so far away!"

The fear was evident in his quivering voice as he repeatedly called out to us. After several hours of anxious searching, we called it a night. I knew from what Zak had told me, along with the bright red frothy blood, that the little buck could not have gone far. It was also evident that daylight would be a great asset in our recovery.

The next morning we found Zak's buck thirty yards from the base of his tree! He was literally lying in the crick. The buck had double backed on his own trail and we had literally walked right by him in the dark the night before. Sadly, a mink had found the buck during the night and ate his nose off. This made the pictures less than a magazine cover worthy, but the taste of success could not have been sweeter.

Fast forward three years. Mark was now deer hunting with me behind Tony's house. Things were going great until the wolves started to howl. Mark was sitting on the ground in a bottleneck. He was located directly between the alpha wolf and the rest of the pack! To say he was a little uneasy was a gross understatement. I was sitting in a tree stand fifty yards away when Mark came and sat beneath me. The next afternoon's sit led to more wolves, followed by more anxiety over a possible encounter. Fear was stealing Mark's peace and joy. Time for Dad to "train up his child in the way he should go" with a little attitude adjustment or maybe just some reprogramming.

Back at the house, I asked Mark, "What kinda gun do you have there?"

"A .35 Remington," he replied.

"Hmmm, are you a good shot?" I asked.

"Yes, you know I am!" he replied with a little attitude.

"How many bullets you got there?"

"A whole box!" he said.

After a brief pause, I asked him, "So what are you afraid of?"

Mark pondered the question for a few moments, and then his eyes lit up. A big smile came across his face, and he said, "Yeah! What am I afraid of!"

Mark's fear of wolf encounters was instantly changed to a hopeful expectation of a wolf encounter. Adrenaline flow would now be processed from flight to fight in his little body. Instead of fear holding him back, he had the confidence to march out boldly with a "go ahead and make my day" attitude.

The most common phrase in the Bible is, "Do not fear," but at the same time, we are told to have a reverent fear of God. Have you ever wondered why God hates our fear of things and circumstances so much? The answer is really quite simple—because when we fear, we are putting more faith in bad circumstances or the devil's ability to harm us than we are in God's ability to provide and protect us. Fears are literally an insult to God! We are telling God we don't trust Him.

Hebrews 13:5 promises, "He will never leave you nor forsake you." Where are you placing your faith? In your strength? In your health, your wealth, your job, your family, your friends? All these things will pass away, but our eternal God will never pass away!

Do you believe the many promises of God contained within his word? Those promises include the provision of His spiritual armor listed out in Ephesians 6:10–17. I guarantee that His armor is better than any old .35 Remington and all the ammo in the world!

Choose to walk in faith today, and leave all your fears at the foot of the cross. God is for you. Take a moment now to pause and remember back to all those impossible situations you've faced in your life. Hindsight is twenty/twenty, and since you're reading this today, you have made it through them all. He was faithful then, and he is faithful now. Take a moment and thank him for his deliverances of old and for how he will deliver you again. All you have to do is ask.

CHAPTER 4

Walking in the Dark

It was 1968 when my dad returned from a Montana elk hunt with a large six-by-six elk rack. I'd love to say Dad had shot that bull, but the reality is, the only bull Dad ever shot was around the dining room table. That bull was actually given to Dad by my mom's cousin Chug, who owned the ranch Dad had been hunting on. Chug had taken many such bulls and was happy to share his wealth.

When Dad pulled into our driveway, I was about as excited as any three-year-old could be. Dad had that huge rack and a nice mule deer buck strapped to the top of our old station wagon. Dad hung the big elk rack in the boys' room, where it stayed from that point on. The boys' room was a basement bedroom I shared off and on with my two older brothers.

I dreamed nightly of the time I would get a chance to harvest such a magnificent beast. Hardly a day went by when I wouldn't run my hands over those long points and heavy beams and say, "Someday."

My chance finally came with a four-year stint in Colorado Springs as an environmental health specialist in the USAF. Although my sole purpose in joining the air force was to go out west hunting on Uncle Sam's dollar, the only trophies I actually came back to Wisconsin with was a mule deer buck and my new bride. The buck was nothing special, but my wife was in a class by herself and was well worth the trip. She still is, for that matter. Although I came up short in harvesting an elk, I did glean a ton of knowledge from my time in the Colorado Rockies.

In 1990 I traveled back to my old stomping grounds with a coworker named Eric. Anticipation filled the thin air as we tried all my best tricks and spots, all to no avail. We had several close calls but just could not seem to close the deal. One afternoon we decided our lungs and legs had adjusted well enough to the elevation to climb up Del Norte. Del Norte is a bald-headed mountain with an elevation of 12,400 feet.

Our climb wasn't for the spectacular views but to reach a bowl just above timberline. The bowl was filled with a mixture of berry brush and shrubs. The bald face in the background made it a perfect amphitheater for calling. Our plan was to start calling about five in the evening and then work our way back down the mountain as darkness approached.

After a two-and-a-half-hour hike up the mountain, we were finally able to settle in for our evening hunt. I had chosen to sit with my back to the bowl, as I tucked in behind a little bush. Any elk entering the bowl from either side I would certainly spot. Eric was set up in front of me about thirty yards away, just on the other side of a dense pine hedge. Both of us were overlooking some heavily used game trails. We were blessed with a nice crosswind that dragged our scent out across the open bowl.

Once settled, I made some random cow calls with my diaphragm mouth call with no response. As we waited, we were treated to an absolutely beautiful view. The Colorado Rockies are truly spectacular! The view alone was well worth the climb. After a few minutes, I let out some more cow calls and followed them up with a lone bugle.

I waited about fifteen minutes and repeated the process, this time adding a chuckle at the end of my bugle. Off in the distance, a lone bugle arose from the southeast. Cool! Game on! This is what makes hunting so much fun—the excitement and anticipation of what might happen. All the questions run through your mind as your heart races. Will he come in? Will he wind me? Will I get a shot? Will I make a good shot? How will we ever get him off of this mountain? The answers to these questions would just have to play out. It's all part of the game.

After waiting a few more minutes, I repeated the process. He immediately responded, and it sounded as if he had cut the distance in half.

As we bugled back and forth, my heart rate was through the roof. Being over eleven thousand feet didn't help either. The bull and I bantered on, back and forth, sounding like a couple of bickering schoolboys on a playground. After about a half hour, he committed and I soon heard hooves on the rocky trail below us. His raggedy, heavy breathing left my knees shaking! It didn't take long before I could see the dense pine branches moving. My mind raced with a mixture of anticipation and questions. Would I get a shot? Why hadn't Eric shot? The bull surely must have almost stepped on him.

As quickly as those random thoughts crossed my mind, they were gone as the branches started to part. With my bow up and ready to draw, out stepped not only one but two big, ugly, stupid, white-faced beef cows. What a kick in the guts! What a tease! What on earth were they doing up that high? In frustration, I pelted one with a rock. That foolish behavior sent them crashing back down the mountain. Not exactly the smartest move on my part! But talk about a letdown.

After a quick powwow with Eric, we decided to start working our way toward the area we had last heard the bull. We set up in some blow downs and began calling again. Amazingly, a bull immediately answered. It took a little coaxing, but he again started working his way toward us. Darkness was closing in fast, but so was the bull.

As darkness fell on us like a blanket, my mind waffled between getting a shot at the bull and our long walk out. The five-by-five bull finally made it to within bow range just as it got too dark to shoot. Although I had a decent thirty-yard shot, I just wasn't comfortable with the lack of shooting light available to make a good shot. I watched in awe and frustration as he slowly slipped away.

Then came the fun part. We still had to get off the mountain in the dark. It had taken us about two and a half hours to hike up the mountain in the daylight following game trails. Now we found ourselves off the game trails in the dark timber. The blow downs and the evergreens were so thick you could hardly walk or see through them. It was literally so black in there you couldn't see three feet in front of you.

Each step was labored as branches were constantly scratching our faces and grabbing at our gear. The only thing we had going for us was it was all downhill. We knew we would eventually hit the logging road that paralleled the ridge if we kept heading downhill. I had taken the lead because I knew where I was headed. But after a while, the branches pulled some of my arrows from my quiver. I stopped to put them in again for the third time when Eric offered to take the lead.

After what seemed like an eternity of following Eric down the mountain, we eventually broke out into the moonlight. I hollered, "Eric, stop!" But it was too late! I knew from experience the only break in the trees was the road that was cut into the side of the mountain twenty feet below us. I knew I should have been leading. I knew I should have at least warned him of the upcoming danger.

Too often both in hunting as well as life, we follow confident, well-intentioned people. They're convinced they know what's best, and it's often easier to let them blaze a path than to pull out the mini mag hiding in your fanny pack and lead them!

Jesus said in Luke 6:39, "A blind man cannot guide a blind man can he? Will they both not fall into a pit?" (NASB).

Jesus is the light of the world, and as believers, we have his light within us. Psalm 119:105 says, "Your word is a lamp to my feet and a light to my path."

We hardly used our flashlights that night because it was so thick you couldn't see more than a few feet anyway, so we feared getting disoriented. Logic said to just keep heading downhill. But our lights would have prevented us from getting scratched, falling down, and losing arrows.

Sometimes it may seem awkward or not worth it to follow God's word or "His light" (the Holy Spirit within believers). Why even bother? Maybe it is easier to follow the crowd. But unseen cliffs do lay ahead. Maybe leaving the light of Christ turned off in your life seems more convenient, even easier, but Jesus does know what's best for us, whether it seems right or not. Why not choose to follow Jesus today and let him be your leader rather than following those in the world?

What happened to Eric? Well, after a lot of grunting, groaning, thumping, and words I never heard in Sunday school, I heard his shaky voice rise up from below: "I saved my bow!"

CHAPTER 5

Zak's "Church" Hat

The 2018 turkey season began much like late bow season had ended—cold, windy, and snowy. But praise the Lord! That meant no mosquitoes or ticks! I was blessed to have drawn the first week of the Wisconsin turkey season. The first week begins on the third Wednesday of April and runs through the following Tuesday. Wisconsin allows a hunter one week a year to run a shaft through a wary bird.

There are a total of five weeklong seasons. But you must apply for the week you desire to hunt in the previous December. This effectively spreads out the hunting pressure. The first season gives you the best crack at an uneducated bird but also opens up the possibility of encountering the worst weather.

Opening morning found us in the ground blind I had set up a few weeks earlier for the youth hunt. The temperatures were in the twenties that morning, with twenty-mile-an-hour winds from the northeast. We were situated along a cut cornfield tucked in along some planted pines that served as a nice windbreak. I had set out a jake and a hen decoy about five yards in front of our blind. The jake was actually an old plastic hen I had found. I modified it by painting its head red, adding a short beard, and screwing on some previously harvested turkey wings and fan. It was awesome looking, and I guess you could say it was an original transgender turkey.

About seven o'clock in the morning, my calling had drawn in a nice tom from across the field from the south. It was a textbook hunt as he walked right up to twenty-five yards away. I cautiously drew my new Mathews Halon 32 back as I waited for the right shot. But instead of continuing into the decoys, he stopped and just stared at my setup with a puzzled look. He then changed directions and walked off into the pines.

I looked down as I wondered what had gone wrong. I could've made the shot, but I had a self-imposed twenty-yard limit due to the strong winds and a turkey's small vital area. Bowhunting is about getting close, after all. Looking down at the decoys, I was surprised to see the strong winds had flipped the hen up on her nose and had torn off one of the jake's wings. I guess God was telling me it was time to head to work!

The next morning I awoke to about an inch of frozen slush beneath three inches of fresh snow. You have got to love spring in Wisconsin—just another wonderful day in paradise! As we made our way back to the pop-up blind in the north, multiple gobbles could be heard sounding off in the south woods. My preferred way to hunt turkeys is to run and gun. I usually walk out behind the barn, hoot like an owl, and then head toward the nearest gobbles. I then try to sneak to within a hundred yards or so, set up, and call to the rooster birds.

This year was different, though. I was really determined to hunt with my bow, so I felt regulated to hunt out of a ground blind, even though I really don't like using them. As I approached my blind, I could see the snow and ice had really done a number on it. The roof had collapsed, and some of the poles were broken. The morning before, in anticipation of the possibility of snow, I had placed an adjustable shooting stick in the center of the blind. I felt this would help support the possible weight of the impending snow, but the shooting stick had also snapped in half.

I climbed inside the collapsed blind and pushed the roof up to clear the frozen mess off, and it made an awful racket. As I forced the roof up and down, trying to free the blind from the ice buildup, one of the broken poles stabbed me in the forehead! I never noticed the profuse amounts of blood coming from my head because I was sweating like a pig from my P90X workout. As my wife often says, "And you call that fun?" Have you ever had one of those days?

The blind was useless in its present condition, and I felt like the area was also ruined after all the noise I had made. After a quick prayer of, "What should I do now, Lord?" Zak and I headed off to where we had heard the toms gobbling in the south. It was time to run and gun with my bow.

I'll admit, I really struggled to get out of bed that morning. With the cold temps and the snow, it just didn't feel like spring turkey season. Now it seemed as if everything had gone wrong. My spirits were pretty low as I second-guessed my decision to go out that morning. But I know full well that I will never harvest an animal from my office chair, the couch, or my bed, so no matter how remote my chances were, I had to keep trying.

As we walked through the cut cornfield, a plan was developing. We would set up the jake over the hen in a mating position. They would be placed a few yards in front of a logging road that entered the cut cornfield. Their positioning would almost guarantee that any turkey crossing the road or entering the field would see the setup.

I would stand facing the field with a large oak at my back. The decoys were ten yards in front of me, with the logging road two yards off to my right. I figured there was a pretty low percentage chance of this actually working, but it beat going home empty-handed. I was hoping that if a tom was strutting, it just might give me an opportunity to get my bow drawn.

Standing up and holding my bow limited me to using only my diaphragm mouth call. As I yelped occasionally on the call, I watched in wonder as the sun crested the hill to the east, illuminating the snowy, cut corn field. The bright sun shining on the field gave the appearance of diamonds glistening in the snow. This was way better than sleeping in!

At seven o'clock, I slowly peeked around the tree and spotted a nice tom working his way down the road. I slowly turned back so the tree would cover my movements. I turned on my lid cam and snapped my release onto the string loop. My body trembled as I could hear the tom strutting, his wingtips dragging along the frozen path. I was afraid to move and couldn't look for fear of him spooking. I had to wait for him to walk by me a scant three yards away! He must have either picked me out or caught some slight movement, because as soon as he got even with me, he spooked, bolting past the decoys and out into the field. I drew my bow in hopes that he would stop, but he just kept running, sounding off as he circled back into the woods. We laughed. Shot or no shot, close encounters like this is why we bowhunt!

I continued to call in hopes that another opportunity might present itself. Twenty minutes later, we again caught movement coming up the road. This time, three nice toms were heading my way. The first two were in a race toward my setup. They passed by me quickly as they ran up and attacked the decoys. The third tom had caught my movement as I drew my bow and quickly ran off to the east.

The two brothers stuck like glue to each other. As they ripped the wing off my Jake and knocked the hen over. Perplexed at the weird lovers they had encountered, they hesitated just long enough for me to settle my top sight pin on the closest tom. My arrow split the gap perfectly between the tree and a vine anchoring the tom to the cornfield.

The other tom ran off as I hollered, "Praise the Lord! Thank you, Jesus!"

I was high-fiving Zak as praise rose from my lips. I could not believe what had just happened! I had been a coin toss away from not even going out that morning. The difficult situations gave me every reason to quit and go home. But I stuck it out and kept trying.

We accomplished a bucket list item, and I couldn't have been happier or more excited.

On my head was Zak's beat-up, camo ball cap. He often referred to this cap as his church hat. I had vowed a few months earlier that I would wear his hat on every hunt that year. I was determined to take Zak on all the hunts we had previously only dreamed of sharing together. You see, three months earlier, my oldest son, Zak, went home to be with the Lord. Now he could only be with me in spirit.

Over the years I've read many hunting magazine articles written about lost loved ones. To be honest, I could only vaguely relate to them. There's a lot of speculation and wishful thinking out there in those stories. My desire has always been to know the truth.

Jesus said, "and you will know the truth, and the truth will make you free"(John 8:32). Hebrews 11 mentions many great heroes of the faith. Hebrews 12:1 follows it up by saying that those men and women of faith comprise a great cloud of witnesses that surround us. Many of us have felt Zak's presence since his passing, while many others have had dreams and visions of him. What we know for sure from scripture is that if you don't trust in Jesus as your Savior, you will die in your sins (John 8:24).

The gospels actually use the word believe over a hundred times in reference to salvation. He who believes in Jesus will live even if he dies (John 11:25). I know Zak lives! I admit, I really don't know if he is confined to heaven or free to hunt with his old man, but I am certain he is alive because of his faith. So whether he's with me in spirit or in my own wishful thinking, he will always be one of my beloved hunting partners. Our adventures will continue even if they may have to be put on hold for a few years till I can join him.

My faith assures me of being reunited with my believing loved ones. What does your faith assure you of?

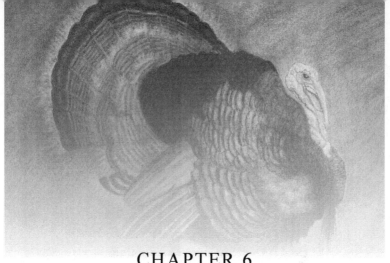

CHAPTER 6

Nick's Turkey

God has blessed my wife and me with three wonderful sons. He has also given us many "adopted" kids that we've mentored through the years. For the most part, we all share a love of the outdoors that helps bond us together. We absolutely love hunting or simply being out in God's beautiful creation.

Well, there always seems to be one exception to any rule, and that exception is my middle son, Nick. He is by far my most passive sportsman. Although he does enjoy hiking, camping, and hanging out in the mountains, he just doesn't have the same drive to harvest animals as the rest of us do. I know it's hard to believe people like that exist, but really they do! While his brothers were filling the freezer in their early teens, Nick was busy playing video games. Although he had successfully beat many levels and won countless battles, his walls remained pretty barren when it came to antlers and heart hair! Nick was twenty years old when his .30-06 finally connected on his first buck.

For Nick, hunting was a social event, a chance to hang out with family and friends and enjoy a walk in the woods. In his eyes, hunting should be more like fishing—you know, catch and release.

After all, if you keep it or shoot it, then you have to clean it. This is kind of ironic, because Nick loves his rotations in both the ER and the OR.

A few years back, I had set my mind on helping Nick get his first turkey. Since time with our adult children is usually pretty limited, I wanted to take advantage of the time we had together. I believe making memories should be a priority in all of our relationships.

Nick had just graduated from college with a bachelor's degree in biology. He was back living at home while working second shift at local surgery center as he awaited acceptance into a PA school. This worked out great, as it allowed us to spend time together and gave us mornings free to turkey hunt.

That first morning we set up on a rolling oak ridge in the predawn darkness. A stubble field lay just to our south, and our decoys were twenty yards out in front of us to the west. An open, mature hardwoods with a small creek lay to the north and east. As we sat down together with our backs against a large oak, I thanked the Lord for this special blessing I was enjoying.

Toms gobbled relentlessly to the west as dawn was breaking. It was a beautiful day, and I just knew we would taste success that day. Turkeys started to fly down from their roosts as our anticipation heightened. Each cluck and purr I made was immediately answered by thunderous gobbles. Today would certainly be Nick's day!

After a few minutes, we noticed a flock of about thirty birds working through the stubble field moving from west to east. The birds managed to stay just out of range. We were set up about twenty yards from the field, and they were thirty yards into the field. Fifty yards is too far for a shot, and the noisy, dry leaves prevented us from any possibility of sneaking any closer. I've had to learn and relearn that there's no such thing as a sure thing.

The next morning was a repeat of the first with the exception of Nick setting up out in front of me and much closer to the field. Again the birds stayed just out of range, passing a little bit further out in the field.

The next hour passed slowly in an unmemorable fashion. Then the distinct sound of footsteps in the leaves snapped us back into reality. Expecting turkeys to appear, we were surprised when a bachelor group of bucks passed by on a game trail less than ten yards away. What a thrill to have these magnificent animals walk by us. They were totally unaware that the world's two greatest predators were sitting motionless within spitting distance. Hmmm, don't buy that? Well how about two average nimrods sitting motionless under a tree with a favorable wind direction? Well either way, it will be forever etched in our memories.

Every day we tried adjusting our locations and setups. Every day we were blessed with close encounters by various large and small animals as well as great father-son moments. Every day we saw toms, yet we were never able to squeeze off a shot. On two separate occasions we had toms well within shooting range, but they just never offered Nick a decent shot.

After a week of working second shift and 4:30 a.m. wakeup calls, Nick's enthusiasm was really starting to wane. On several occasions, I had to throw things at Nick to alert him that toms were coming. I could never be certain if he was awake or not. Between the flying acorns and Nick's snoring, the toms somehow managed to keep avoiding us. Hmmm, go figure.

When the last day finally arrived, it was wet, cold, and dreary. Our previous tom encounters brought us back to our old, familiar ridge. By nine o'clock in the morning, our old, familiar ridge brought only old, familiar results. The once-loud and crunchy leaves were now wet and silent. This quiet walking, allowed a silent tom to sneak in undetected—although I must say, he was very vocal as he ran away after spotting Nick readjusting his backside.

I suggested to Nick that we try a quick setup at a different farm on our way home. Nick reluctantly agreed. Our new spot was a secluded cut cornfield surrounded by woods and valleys. We had set up directly on the edge of the field with our backs against one of my favorite bow stands. My yelps and purrs brought immediate responses from several directions. Cool, game on!

Soon the largest tom I have ever seen stepped out. He crossed the field at about fifty yards. Nick's maximum range with his twelve-gauge is forty yards. I tried unsuccessfully to call him closer, but after a few moments the big tom decided he wanted nothing to do with us and continued strutting out across the field. Ten yards may not sound like much, but at that range, your shot pattern can really spread out, leaving a wounded bird to run off and become coyote food.

More calling produced two more toms coming up from a different direction. They strutted and gobbled all the way across the field, only to hang up about fifty yards away. Some hens had intercepted them and proceeded to lead the boys away to the other end of the field. We were frustrated. It seemed we just couldn't buy a break. Time was running out. It was time to get aggressive!

We decided to drop into the valley and follow it undetected to just below the other end of the field. Our new setup would put us just below the birds. Settling in, I started to call as we watched the ridge above us for one of those toms to drop in. A hen launched my heart into my throat when she snuck in from behind and busted us at five yards. She noisily let everything in the country know of her displeasure as she ran away.

Discouraged, but still optimistic, we decided to try a small island woods for one last attempt. The rain was coming down much harder now, and the birds weren't talking or moving. Reluctantly, we decided to call it quits. We were slowly trudging back to the truck through a cut corn field, soaked to the bone, cold and dejected. We really had nothing to be ashamed of. We had given it our best shot but still had nothing to show for all our efforts.

The cut cornfield was covered with thick, freshly spread manure. *Perfect*, I thought. *How fitting.* What a perfect end to a perfect season. As we crested a rise in the field, my truck appeared about a 150 yards out on the horizon. To my surprise and delight, a flock of turkeys also appeared between the truck and us. Thank you, Lord! We just might score after all!

I immediately told Nick to drop. We then belly crawled as close as we dared through the wet and muddy manure. Using the rise in the field as cover, I had Nick belly crawl another ten yards in front of me as I raised a decoy and started calling. It didn't take long before a pair of legal jakes appeared and walked within ten yards in front of Nick. Nick was lying on his belly with his gun to his shoulder as they passed by.

I watched excitedly as I plugged my ears, waiting for his gun to fire. Shoot! Come on, shoot! Come on, man! What are you waiting for? I continued to talk to myself as the birds continued to waddle off. They continued to bob and weave until they were over forty yards away. That's when I screamed, "Shoot already!"

Boom! Click, click! Boom! Birds scattered everywhere as we jumped to our feet. After our long search only revealed a few feathers, I asked Nick, "What on earth were you waiting for?"

He replied, "I saw a tom in with the flock, and I thought you'd get mad if I shot a jake."

I laughed and pointed at the truck less than a hundred yards away. "Nick, it's the last minute of the last day. It was our last chance. The truck is right there! We are both cold, wet, hungry, and covered with manure! Nick, sometimes you just have to take what the Lord gives you! Let's go eat. I'm hungry."

Some would consider Nick's turkey hunt a waste of time and sleep. But Nick? He considered it his best and most memorable hunt ever. I firmly believe that the joy is truly in the journey and not in the destination. The apostle Paul wrote in Philippians 4:11 "that he had learned to become content in all circumstances". Paul had certainly experienced much worse than belly crawling through wet manure! But through all of his trials, he kept his eyes focused on the prize of the upward call of God in Christ Jesus (Philippians 3:14).

There is a real peace and joy to know your father is with you and is pleased with you, despite whatever crap you may be crawling through. It doesn't matter whether you're successful in the world's eyes or not. As children of the king, we can be content in the Lord no matter what. He is for you, he is with you, and he does love you! Focusing on his love for us and just being with him makes the seemingly worst of times the best of times. Just ask Nick!

CHAPTER 7

Power of the Tongue

James 3:2 states, "We all stumble in many ways, if anyone does not stumble in what he says he's a perfect man and able to bridle the whole body as well." Boy, am I not perfect! My mouth has gotten me into a lot of trouble over the years. My quick wit is combined with a filter that … ahh, we could say was often used for target practice. It has sharpened my fight-or-flight response to a razor's edge. Praise the Lord! As I aged, I came to the realization that I had two ears and one mouth for a reason.

As I learned to call animals, I had to apply the same principle of listening more than I speak to my calling. Less is more! The right word in the right circumstances is much better than many wrong words or actions in any circumstance! The old KISS principle (keep it simple stupid) definitely applies here. Let me share some examples.

A friend of mine and I were waiting for the perfect wind, combined with a day off to rattle a bottleneck on a particular forty. There was a big wide twelve pointer hanging out there. We would need to hunt from the ground in a patch of tag alders, so the right wind was crucial.

The day before our big hunt, my friend snuck into his nearby tree stand for an evening hunt. Soon afterward, he watched two farm boys race across the field on a four-wheeler. One was dropped off while the other one returned home. Before the driver was even out of sight, the hunter began beating two horns together relentlessly. He continued to beat them together for forty-five minutes. That's when his brother returned to pick him up for the evening chores. Needless to say, I would guess he came to the conclusion that rattling doesn't work.

Another time I was hunting the famed Musselshell River of Montana for elk. We had set up along a ridge overlooking the river and farm fields. The elk would often feed in the fields all night long and then work their way back to the high country to bed in the morning. Sitting quietly downwind of one of the numerous trails is usually your best bet to harvest an animal. These animals are heavily hunted and very cautious. Calling will often only alert them to your presence.

On one particular morning, a herd of about thirty elk trotted over the ridge about a quarter of a mile north of my location. I watched in horror and total disbelief as some nimrod jumped up and began chasing the herd across the bald ridge, as he squealed away frantically on a cow call. As my dad would say, "And then they shot men like Lincoln!"

Calling or talking to an animal requires the right words in the right situation. A bugle or the wrong bugle can often send a herd bull running away from you. Keep in mind that a bugle is a challenge. You're telling him, "I'm here. I'm not afraid of you. I want to kick your butt and steal your girlfriend!" With that in mind, would you risk it? Or would you quietly climb into your car with your wife and drive away?

That's the very thing that happened to me a few years ago. My son and a good friend of mine both had bull tags, while I was pretty much just along for the ride. I guess I also came along for some comic relief, to call and help pack out if necessary.

We had chosen what I thought was a perfect location. We set up in a large, relatively open park dotted with sporadic jack pines. There were a lot of fresh elk signs, and we were really stoked. Mark and Tony spread out in front of me as I set up Miss September (our decoy) behind them on a little knob. I was tucked in some cover about seventy yards behind the guys. I let out a bugle and followed it up with some cow calls. I was shocked at how quickly and close the response came. The response happened to be a guy on a four wheeler! The mile-long hike to our perfect setup? Well, it turned out to be just twenty yards short of an ATV trail. Sigh ...

After a quick discussion, we packed up and started hiking back toward the truck. Tony suggested I bugle off the edge of a deep ravine. This was just a few yards from where I had been just calling from. I reluctantly agreed, and to my surprise, a deep, growling bugle responded. We stared at each other in disbelief. I waited a few minutes before bugling again to try and pinpoint his location. His unmistakable bugle erupted from the side of the ridge only a few hundred yards away. The ridge was incredibly steep, and there was no way for us to safely go down it, nor did I believe the big bull would leave his cows to billy goat up to us.

Our only choice would be to run back along the park as we paralleled the ridge. It was about a half-mile jaunt before the terrain would allow us to drop down to an old logging road. We would then use the road to get the wind in our favor as we cut the distance. Our goal was to sneak in close enough to him that he felt threatened enough to turn and fight.

After we had snuck in as close as we dared, we chose our ambush spots. In the process, the guys stumbled across two monster muleys. Amazingly, the bucks just stood there looking at them from twenty yards away. Folks, just a word to the wise—always have an arrow nocked when you've closed the distance on your quarry. You never know what or when something might happen. After watching the guys as they fumbled to nock an arrow, the bucks simply trotted off.

My first bugle received an immediate response from less than a hundred yards away. After waiting a few minutes, my second bugle produced a response out closer to 250 yards. This big bull wanted no part of me, and he headed up and over the mountain, taking his harem with him. Ironically, what drove the big boy away was drawing in his little buddy.

A satellite bull had left the herd and was now screaming back and forth with me. I matched his pitch and intensity while throwing in a variety of cow calls. My challenger ventured into range several times but always stayed in the thick cover. Back and forth we paralleled each other as we each tried to stay upwind of the other. We played this game of chess until darkness finally overcame us. That dirty little critter never did offer the guys a shot.

The very sounds or words that turned one bull away drew another one in. Our speech often does the very same thing. What might make your buddy laugh hysterically could be a major turnoff to others. I'm willing to bet your best friend and your mother in law do not have the same sense of humor. Whether we are dealing with humans or animals, the goal is to match your calling or speech with the situation or audience. I've found that sometimes our calling can be downright dangerous. I've had wolves and bears literally run into the sound of rattling horns.

Here are a couple of examples of when calling has gotten me into trouble. Many years ago, I was bowhunting whitetails near the Trapp River in north central Wisconsin. The only tree anywhere near where I wanted to hunt was rather small and had a lot of limbs. This limited me to only getting about six to eight feet off the ground with my climbing tree stand. The tree was located between a creek and a cut corn field.

To my surprise, my first rattling sequence brought a nice black bear in on the run. After he stopped about thirty yards away, I grunted at him just to observe his response. I was amazed when he ran to the base of my tree, stood on his hind legs, and began sniffing around. I could have literally kicked him in the nose! One good snout full of my scent and he looked like a bowling ball shot out of a cannon as he headed for parts unknown.

I would not consider myself a nervous or fearful man, although I did get a little anxious a while back. My wife and I were driving down a gravel road outside of Spokane, Washington. It was the beginning of October, and the moose rut was in full swing. The fall colors were spectacular as we drove around that evening enjoying the scenery and looking for game. I soon spotted a bull moose feeding in an island of willows about 150 yards away. I pulled the truck over, and we got out, armed only with our binoculars and cell phones.

I thought it would be great to get a better look at him, so I let out a few cow calls. That certainly got his attention! So I let out another cow call and followed it up with a couple of bull grunts. That was all it took. He was on his way! We were excitedly taking pictures and videos of him as he stopped to destroy a willow about seventy-five yards away. One more cow call should do it. By the way, a cow call is a mournful, bellowing sound a cow moose makes when she is in heat. It's her version of saying, "I'm naked, and I've got a pizza!"

That did it. The big bull picked up his pace as he moved quickly toward us. It was then that I noticed my wife was wearing a big black hoodie. I also noticed the bull's tongue was hanging out as he licked his lips. I told my wife to quickly get in the truck. She ignored my request and kept taking pictures. I insisted; she argued! I pleaded with my excited wife, who was happily enjoying her time with me on one of my adventures.

Now moose are not known for their keen eyesight. And just like that old Johnny Lee song, this old boy was looking for love in all the wrong places. This bull was heading straight for my bride with his tongue hanging out.

Now after much thoughtful consideration, I have come to the conclusion that there is no good way of telling your wife she looks like a moose. So I abandoned the argument and jumped in the truck. I drove forward as I cut the bull off. He was less than twenty yards away at the time.

This great act of chivalry did not delight my lovely wife, as I had hoped, as it apparently ruined her chances of very close-up pictures.

She was even less delighted when I explained that more people are killed in Alaska every year by moose than they are by grizzlies and wolves combined.

A vibrant conversation then ensued, with my wife questioning me as to why I would choose to use that call, especially if he was going to run at us. I replied with, "Sorry, dear, but I don't know moose for, 'Hey, can you come over here so I can take your picture.' Remember, dear, last week I was chasing a grizzly with a bow just to make sure he wasn't a black bear. With that in mind, if I'm running for the truck, you might want to follow suit! It's really not the time for a debate."

Our calling or words can get us into a heap of trouble. My wife and I can laugh about our moose experience now. It wasn't nearly as funny at the time, or at least she didn't think so. Scripture says that our enemy prowls around like a roaring lion seeking someone to devour. The enemy most often uses our own mouths or words to destroy us.

Sometimes the enemy comes rushing in like that bear I mentioned earlier. Other times he sneaks in downwind like a wolf waiting for a buck to be vulnerable during a breeding battle.

Proverbs 18:21 says that death and life are in the power of the tongue.

James 3:1–12 could be summarized by saying our tongues defile our entire bodies. Our tongues are full of deadly poison. We can choose to use our tongues to either bless or curse others, to build up or tear down. What proceeds from our mouths is really an evidence of what is in our hearts. How will you choose to use your tongue today?

CHAPTER 8

Bottleneck Buck

Whitetail hunters tend to place their stands along corn, bean, or alfalfa fields. After all, that's the way they do it on TV! It seems most of us have watched video after video of monster bucks coming into these fields during daylight hours, only to get whacked from above by some super hunter. The buck then races off and expires in the lush crops, where the mighty hunter can conveniently drive up to Bullwinkle with his truck or quad. A photo shoot then ensues, complete with toothy grins as they kneel behind the fallen monarch. His antlers look almost fake, they are so huge.

The reality is, most of us can only watch and dream of winning that lottery. Instead we head out to the back forty in hopes of catching a glimpse of a Price County eleven-pointer, also known as a spike or cow horn.

Midwest farm country does produce the huge deer we all dream about. But truth be told, most of us simply don't live in farm country. Even those of us who do probably don't have access to those well-managed properties.

I have lived most of my life in the big, forested lands of northern Wisconsin. Instead of cornfields we had poplar slashings. Tag alder swamps replace alfalfa fields, and few up there have ever even heard of soybeans. There are just miles upon miles of swamps and woods with few roads to split them up. A compass is your lifeline. Patterning deer? Seriously? Not a chance, when their diet mostly consists of random twigs. The idea of sitting in your truck with a spotting scope, as you drink coffee and watch where your buck enters the field? Forget it!

So how do you effectively hunt the north woods? Well, the options are limited, but there are options. Oak ridges are the ticket— that is, if you happen to have oaks. The reality is much of the north woods are lowlands filled with conifer swamps. This makes tasty acorns pretty hard to come by. Some people plant apple trees or food plots. If you have the time, money, and more importantly, the land, these are great options.

Again, most of us simply don't have any of these. Where legal, baiting is an option. This also requires time and money, but it also rubs some folks the wrong way. Truth be told, you will seldom see anything bigger than a yearling buck coming into bait during daylight hours, so baiting is anything but a guarantee of success.

My hands-down favorite way to hunt is to call animals. But calling is often limited to only a few good weeks a year. Now when you combine calling with a natural funnel? Then you have a winning ticket as the odds swing in your favor. Funnels are also frequently referred to as bottlenecks. Bottlenecks are areas that squeeze deer through a narrow space as they wander from one woods to another. Beaver ponds, rivers, roads, and swamps can all channel or funnel a deer's movements. If you find one of these areas, then you can make a plan to intercept them.

One of my favorite bottleneck stands was located about ten feet up a maple tree. This tree was less than a foot in diameter. I know I stuck out like a sore thumb in that tree, but it really was my only choice, as it was the only tree big enough to support a tree stand. The bare-branched tree was sandwiched between two huge beaver ponds. The ponds were only about fifty yards apart. In front of me was a hundred-acre poplar slashing. Each of the poplar trees were only about an inch and a half in diameter. Behind me was a large tag alder swamp that eventually transitioned into a mature forest.

It was a perfect early November afternoon, cool and overcast. There was a slight westerly breeze blowing in my face. I was facing the young poplar growth that spread out before me. Their branches were barren, and the ground was carpeted with their golden leaves. As much as I desired to hunt that afternoon, I was just as anxious for the clouds to clear off so I could watch the sunset over this unique landscape.

I picked up my rattling horns and cracked them together, breaking the afternoon silence. I twisted the horns together as I ground the beams and tickled the tines against each other. This process only took about a minute and a half. After hanging my horns up, I quickly grabbed my bow. Years of experience had taught me a buck could appear at any moment. I've watched many bucks sneak in cautiously, while others literally run in. You just never know, so you have to be ready!

A buck soon appeared, coming toward me from the northwest. He would stop periodically to make a scrape or rub his antlers. There is no possible way to sneak an arrow through a poplar slashing. It is way too thick with the little trees weaved together like a cheap rug. The buck would have to step out onto the game trail for me to have any chance for a shot.

At twenty yards, he stopped to make yet another scrape when he noticed me. How could he not! There was simply no cover in that tree, and I must have looked like a half-eaten lollipop in that skinny tree. He stared and stared for several minutes before turning to leave. I grunted, and he came to a halt. He looked back briefly before continuing on. I grunted again, but this time I followed it up with a doe in heat bleat.

I make all my deer vocalizations with my own voice, from grunts to tending grunts, to snort wheezes, to doe-in-heat bleats. If you practice these different calls until you are proficient, you can greatly reduce the amount of movement you have to make. The less you move, the less chance you have of getting busted by a wary whitetail.

The doe-in-heat bleat stopped the buck in his tracks. After a quick 180, he was coming in again. This time he wandered a few yards closer. He again stopped short as he stared at the big blob in the tree. Minutes passed, and he again turned and walked away. The doe bleat stopped him again. Seconds passed, and I let out another bleat. Again he started coming in. This game of yoyo went on for over thirty minutes. The wary buck stayed anywhere from five to thirty yards from my tree but never gave me a shot as he stared at me the entire time. The buck looked determined as he left again. I figured it was game over, but to my surprise, the doe bleat worked again.

For those who may be unaware of what the purpose of a doe-in-heat bleat is, there is a twenty-four-hour period each fall when a doe will cycle or is available for breeding. This whiny bleat is the sound she makes during that time period. This sound lets every buck in earshot know that she's available. Imagine a woman getting on a PA in the local bar or hardware store saying, "I am naked, and I have a pizza!" You get the picture!

Well, this buck must have liked pizza a lot because he was coming in again, staring at me the whole time. But this time he passed directly below me. I just couldn't believe he was that hungry. As soon as his eyes disappeared behind his antlers, I drew back. I carefully picked a spot and shot. I watched expectantly as he crashed off into the slashing for the last time.

I hit him a little far back but knew I had a great angle. I decided to let him sit overnight just to be safe. It was getting late, and I had to teach a hunter safety class that started that evening. I recovered the buck quickly the next morning after a short, forty-yard trailing job. I brought the buck to the hunter safety class that morning, and he was a big hit as the future hunters got some good, hands-on training.

I am often amazed at how driven an animal can be. That buck knew I was there. He could clearly see me as well as sense the danger. He turned and left for freedom and safety multiple times. Each time he was tempted back with the promise of a doe he couldn't see or smell.

Stupid buck, you think? Well, maybe so. But how often do we do the same thing? We see the danger, but we ignore it. We know we should run, fully comprehending that staying will only get us into trouble. But we hang around, flirting with the danger. Maybe we even pretend it's not really that bad. Or we lie to ourselves, telling ourselves that we won't get caught.

Proverbs 7 tells us about a young man lacking sense. He first flirts with and then goes into his neighbor's wife. The story ends in verse 23, with an arrow piercing his liver. Hmmm, that sounds just like my buck! We are all vulnerable to different things. We are all tempted by things that can cost us dearly if we give into them, or they may be things we just continue doing that we know are wrong.

God didn't leave us as orphans. He has offered help!

> No temptation has overtaken you but such as is common to man; and God is faithful, who will not allow you to be tempted beyond what you are able, but with the temptation will provide the way of escape also, so that you will be able to endure it. (1 Corinthians 10:13)

When tempted, we must not ignore it. We must humbly call upon the Lord to help us out of the situation. He will help us through the temptation and back to the safety of the slashing, but we have to ask. Remember, he wants you to succeed! He didn't cause the temptation in the first place.

> Let no one say when he is tempted, "I am being tempted by God"; for God cannot be tempted by evil, and He Himself does not tempt anyone. But each one is tempted when he is carried away and enticed by his own lust. Then when lust has conceived, it gives birth to sin; and when sin is

accomplished, it brings forth death. Do not be deceived, my beloved brethren. Every good thing given and every perfect gift is from above, coming down from the Father of lights, with whom there is no variation or shifting shadow. (James 1:12–17)

Remember, you are a victorious overcomer in Christ Jesus!

CHAPTER 9

Marathon Man

Many of us dream of hunting the vast and rugged mountains of the west. We fantasize about pursuing elk, mule deer, moose, big horns, and goats in the dangerous wilds they call home. We may also feel a little anxious about our physical abilities or inabilities to accomplish such feats. Maybe it's the possibility of getting altitude sickness. Maybe your joints begin to ache at the mere thought of a possible five-mile pack out, a hundred-pound pack throwing you off balance as you descend down steep inclines with one hand on the ground.

To be honest, unless you are a road hunter or you're willing to pay someone a lot of money, mountain hunting is very hard work. You have to be willing to hike ten to twenty miles a day in steep terrain, with limited oxygen. It's really not for the weak of heart. But let's face it, that is really what separates the consistently successful hunters from the dreamers. You have to be willing to ask yourself, "How bad do I really want this? And am I willing to put in the work to make it happen?"

To be in elk shape by September, I try to stay active all year long, but I usually start my cardio workouts in March or April. It really depends on how much snow is still on the roads. Since I'm not a big fan of pain, I start off small. I run about a mile the first day, and then I add a few blocks to my run each day. By the end of June, I'm ready for a half marathon. If I'm feeling really ambitious, by September I can do a full marathon, or at least I could in my younger years.

Marathons may not be on everyone's bucket list, but running is an excellent way to get into elk shape. I never want my health or physical limitations to prevent me from doing what I love or worse— not being able to enjoy what I love.

My morning runs have blessed me with countless gorgeous sunrises. Deer, turkey, bears, foxes, coyotes, wolves, antelope, and elk have all watched me panting down the trails and roads of this great nation. But so far no Sasquatches—at least not yet! This past spring I even found three whitetail sheds while running.

Running is also my favorite prayer time. It's just me and Jesus. Animal sightings are really the only distraction, and that's not a problem either, because Jesus made them, so he thinks they are pretty cool too. Far too often our prayer lives can turn into dull routines or endless laundry lists. Think about it. If you're bored with your prayer life, just think how God must feel. That critter sighting may be God's way of changing the subject. Try praising him for that critter and add a little spontaneity to your prayer life.

One cold, dreary, late-September afternoon, I was preparing for a marathon—a mere 26.2-mile jaunt. It was a Sunday afternoon and my only chance for an extended run. The temperature was in the low-to mid-forties, and I was in shorts and a T-shirt. My plan was to run down an old abandoned railroad track to a small town about thirteen miles away. I would then return on the same route. The pine line, as it's called, runs through some nasty swamps and woods, with very few crossroads.

My run down to town went great. I was making good time, and I felt great. The critters were out and about. I saw one black bear and several deer. I was heading back home when the rain started and the temperature started to plummet. I found myself seriously concerned about the possibility of hypothermia. As the miles dragged on, I hit what runners refer to as hitting the wall.

The wall can happen at any time but usually occurs between miles sixteen and twenty. You feel as if you're running against a hundred-mile-an-hour gale-force headwind. Your feet feel as if someone is holding them down. Each labored step you take, you swear will be your last. You're certain you can't take another step, let alone run another six to ten miles.

I'm anything but anxious or a worrier, but that afternoon, I was seriously concerned about hypothermia and if I would even make it home. My casual conversation with the Lord turned into a fervent plea for help. Every step was very labored, and I was shaking uncontrollably. I pushed on as I begged for help. "Lord, please send a four-wheeler, a horse, a bike, anything to give me a ride! Lord, maybe just someone who could call my wife to come and get me?" This was getting serious.

God answers prayers. It may not always be in the way we hope, but he does answer. That day God didn't send me a quad or a horse. He didn't send me a dirt bike or a cyclist. Instead God sent me something I had never expected.

As I prayed and looked around for someone or something—anything, really—off to my right I spotted three big, mean farm dogs. They were headed straight at me on a dead run, barking, snarling, and growling. The fear of them gave me a much-needed adrenaline rush. I took off in a gear I didn't even know I had. I looked like the FTD florist man. My feet were only touching the ground just long enough to steer. Wow! Where did that burst come from? I went from out of gas and running on fumes to off to the races. The dogs gave up the pursuit after a few hundred yards, but that adrenaline rush sustained me all the way home. I'm amazed at what God can provide us with in a seemingly hopeless situation.

> Do not fear, for I am with you; Do not anxiously
> look about you, for I am your God. I will strengthen
> you, surely I will help you, surely I will uphold you
> with my righteous right hand. (Isaiah 41:10)

What an awesome promise! I have a relationship with the everlasting God, the Creator of this earth and everything in it. God has a plan for me, and he desires that I fulfill it. If I don't fulfill it, it's because I gave up or I made a poor choice. I could've given up and succumbed to hypothermia. I could have been attacked by those dogs. But I chose to press on and clung to God's promise of good for me.

Giving up is easy; pressing on his hard. God will bring you through it. He is there for you! He's also there with you! And he does answer prayers. It may not always be the way you would have hoped for, and it may not be what you expected, but he will bring you through it.

If you're reading this, you have made it through every trial you've ever encountered. Whether you came out of it a victor or a victim usually depends upon how close you hung onto Jesus through it. I was not harmed by the weather, the wall, or the dogs. I finished my course without ever stopping, and I can look back now on how God provided a way when there wasn't a way. He helped me press on when everything I prayed for was an opportunity to give up.

How will God answer your prayers today?

CHAPTER 10

Migration Route Muleys

Have you ever noticed how big little boys' ears can be? Don't get me wrong, they are cute and all, but they can also be a little goofy-looking at the same time. I'm really not sure why their ears tend to stick out so far. I can only guess that it's from their old-school grandmas dragging them around by their ears. The naughtier the boy, the bigger the ears. Hmmm—just something to ponder. My dad would describe these little boys as looking like a taxi cab with both doors open. He would say, "Just look for a pair of ears, and little Billy will be standing right between them."

Most of us eventually grow into our ears, but it seems like mule deer never do. Those massive donkey like ears surely made them the laughingstock of the deer family. Is it possible mule deer have to lay their ears back when they run, just so a strong headwind doesn't flip them over? Maybe that's why mule deer tend to bounce like Tigger, rather than run like a whitetail. Maybe, maybe not. But mule deer have to be proof that God has a sense of humor.

As goofy as mule deer does and little bucks may look, there is something truly incredibly majestic about a big mule deer buck. You know the type, with heavy, wide, sweeping antlers that extend well past those big ears. They have deep, dark forks that glisten in the morning sun. Some of those antlers may even sport the occasional flyer or drop tine, breaking up the rack's symmetry. I get chills just thinking about it!

Most hunters have dreamed of harvesting such a buck! They love to imagine the post-hunt photo shoots, picturing the big buck's antlers sky-lined against a snowy mountain backdrop, their toothy grins displaying the depth of their accomplishment. Oh the adventures that would accompany such a harvest!

It takes a lot of hard work, careful planning, and some blessings from above for our dreams to actually become a reality. But our hoping and dreaming are the best motivators to push our dreams into reality. I truly love the expectation along with the fantasizing and believe they are half the fun as we dream of the upcoming fall. But our fantasies seldom live up to what reality brings us.

A while back, I was talked into applying for a mule deer tag for northwest Wyoming. This region is the same area in which my son Mark used to live and guide. He would call and tempt me with numerous stories and pictures of Boone and Crockett bucks. He loved to sit and watch these monsters as they migrated down from the high country. The deer were headed into the valleys below, where they would spend the winter.

"Dad, you have got to come out here! There are huge bucks all over the place! I guarantee we can get you a buck." You get the picture?

With a January deadline, I conceded and applied for the coveted tag. A month later, I was bummed to hear that the deer population had been devastated by back-to-back four-foot snowfalls. These power dumps had killed over 90 percent of the deer living in the area. After hearing about the winter kill and reading that the number of harvest tags for that area was going to be significantly reduced, I knew I had better make alternate plans. Even if I did somehow manage to draw a tag, it didn't sound as if there would be any deer left to hunt.

My plan B would be a couples' hunt. My wife and I, along with friends Tony and Jane, would travel to the Bozeman area. While there, I would call elk for Tony and Mark while our wives would break in their new camper. This new plan would use up all my vacation time and spending money for the year, but I really enjoy playing guide as well as the fellowship, almost as much as I do carrying a bow myself. I figured the possible sacrifice of a lost hunt would be well worth it.

Needless to say, I was shocked when I received my Wyoming deer tag in the mail! Actually, I was more disappointed than excited. Sadly, I wouldn't be able to get my tag money refunded, and there was no way I could go back out west in November to hunt the migration hunt. Being a man of my word, I was committed to the September vacation in Montana with my family. I was not about to renege! Rather than stressing out about it, I just gave it up to the Lord and figured I would just have to eat that deer tag.

September and October came and went. We all had a great time out west and we were blessed to share some awesome memories together. The guys were also blessed with some close encounters with both bulls and bucks. It didn't seem to matter that neither of the guys were successful in closing the deal on an antlered critter.

The beginning of November found me swapping hunting stories with a friend. That's when the subject of that mule deer tag came up. He was shocked that I never tried to fill my tag. I was even more shocked when he offered me his frequent flyer miles so I could fly out and give it a try. He really wanted to help me make it happen! How could I possibly let him down and say no?

Hmmm? A free plane ticket? The harvest tag was already paid for? Sounded like a no-brainer to me. But I needed to run the opportunity past my boss. After a quick affirmation from my wife, plan C came together quickly—and it had to since the firearms season on deer closes in Wyoming on November 10, which was just a little over a week away.

Plan C entailed me flying to Bozeman on November 7 to pick up Mark. After Mark got off work, we would drive to Cody later that evening. That left us two and a half days to get 'er done. We would have to call it quits by noon on the tenth (Friday) so Mark could get back to work that evening.

Our game plan was simple enough. We would park at the trailhead and ride horses back six to ten miles each morning. We would then set up on a likely crossing and enjoy the scenery as hundreds of mule deer paraded by us. When a monster buck comes by, you simply settle your crosshairs on his shoulder and squeeze the trigger. Let the photoshoot begin! Sounded like a pretty simple plan to me.

Do things ever go according to plan in your world? In my world, reality seldom meets or even parallels my expectations. But even if things didn't go quite right, two and a half days should be plenty of time to get a buck, right? After all, this trip was certainly a gift from God. What could possibly go wrong?

By midmorning on Wednesday the eighth, we were already road hunting. Yes, road hunting! The horses we were counting on fell through, leaving us to hunt on foot in a foot of snow. Although it was not preferable, I was still willing to walk for a buck. But every trailhead we drove to had six to thirty horse trailers parked there ahead of us. Hiking in behind them would be just a waste of time and energy.

No offense, folks, but as far as I'm concerned, road hunting ranks right up there with kissing your sister on the old excito-meter. If that's your idea of being one with nature, more power to you, but it's just not for me. There has got to be another alternative.

As Mark and I drove around drinking coffee and contemplating our options, we were entertained by several herds of elk. Some of these herds numbered over six hundred head. We also spotted around a hundred mule deer and a few dozen big horns. It may sound like a gimme hunt, but virtually all the land in the valley is privately owned. That meant we could look but not touch—kind of like the girls in church youth group.

The valley's landscape was very open and surrounded by rugged snow capped mountains. The only trees or cover to be found were along the Shoshone River. Well, almost the only cover. We did find one small patch of woods. It consisted of two rows of huge planted pines and two rows of big cottonwoods. This sanctuary was about 50 yards wide and 150 yards long. It had a highway on one end and a cabin at the other. But it was literally crawling with deer.

After we secured permission to hunt this refuge, anxiety set in. There was already a tree stand set up for me to use, but the idea of shooting a .30-06 in such close quarters did not sit well with me. I'm a bowhunter at heart, and I needed to find a bow and find it quick. We spent the rest of Wednesday attempting to rent or borrow a bow, with no luck. The best we could come up with was an old crossbow owned by Mark's former coworker. That crossbow would just have to do. After a little practice at the local archery shop, I felt confident with it out to about twenty-five yards.

Thursday morning, Mark dropped me off before daylight, and I snuck into the ladder stand for the morning hunt. As the dawn's colors of pinks and oranges reflected off the snowy ground, deer started to pour into this little wood lot. Before long, I had a dozen deer milling around below me. We had originally planned that I would only sit for a few hours before texting Mark to come and get me. Then we would weigh out our options and possibly try some spot and stalk hunting. Eleven long, cold hours later, the two dozen deer that had been bedded below me all day began to move back into the alfalfa fields. The temperatures had only been in the teens, and I had little food and water. By the day's end, I thought my bladder would explode. Despite all the physical discomfort, it was truly one of the most incredible days I had ever spent hunting. There were as many as twenty-three deer bedded within bow range of me at any given time. I was totally engrossed in the hunt as I witnessed seven different buck fights that day.

That evening, I excitedly told Mark about the day's events as we planned our final morning's hunt. Friday was now upon us, and we would only have until noon to get 'er done! My ultimate desire for this hunt was to spend time with my son. It was not to sit alone in a tree. I had to practically beg Mark to sit with me the next morning.

He really wanted me to score and feared his presence would lessen my chances. But I convinced him to join me by explaining that we would hunt them like turkeys. We would sit with our backs against a big pine tree on the eastern edge of the woods. The west wind blowing in our faces would prevent the deer from smelling us. Besides, it would be an awesome father-son experience even if I didn't score.

As daylight approached, the deer started to filter into our personal game farm. Two bucks started fighting at the far end of the woods. The two-year-olds slowly worked their way toward us as they continued to push and shove one another. After their sparring match was over, they bedded at thirty and twenty-five yards away respectively. A fork horn then joined them, bedding down a mere twenty yards away. Then a big doe decided to bed directly below the ladder stand. She was facing us, and her stare was incredibly unnerving as she was only ten steps away!

The problem was now, with all of those deer staring at us, we could not move a muscle. And our butts were incredibly numb from being wet and frozen in the snow. By 8:30, all of our muscles were really sore from being so tense. I can't understate how seriously uncomfortable we both were. We felt as if we were in some bad Survivor immunity challenge. I finally whispered to Mark, "I'm thinking about shooting the bigger buck bedded at thirty yards." As the minutes ticked by, my butt grew even number, if that was even possible. I really didn't want to shoot that little four-by-four, but he was the biggest buck we had seen and time was running out. Besides, Mark really wanted the meat.

As I contemplated taking the shot, a new buck chased a doe into our woods. I whispered to Mark, "There's a bigger buck coming, and if he gives me a shot, I'm going to take him."

As the buck bumped the other deer to their feet, I slowly raised the crossbow and rested it on my knee. That slight movement sent all the deer already staring at me toward the Mexican border. Thankfully, the buck I wanted was so focused on a doe he never even noticed us. The buck circled around in front of us and stopped broadside at twenty yards. He was busy sniffing his would-be girlfriend when my broadhead passed cleanly through the four-by-four's cage.

I had dreamed of huge bucks with wide, sweeping antlers, deep, dark forks contrasting a snowy backdrop! I dreamed of a backcountry horse hunting adventure complete with grizzly bear sightings. I dreamed of watching parades of deer, followed by a single well-placed shot.

What I was actually blessed with was a thin-horned four-by-four taken with a borrowed crossbow on the last day of gun season. He wasn't the booner I'd always dreamed of, but truth be told, I'd take that unparalleled experience over my fantasy hunt hands down. The best part of it all? My son was shoulder to shoulder with me videotaping the shot with his cell phone.

Dreams? Expectations? Wishful thinking? We all plan out our hunts, as well as our lives. We plan out our families, our vacations, and our careers. But our perfect plans seldom turn out the way we hoped they would. Our choices are then to roll with the punches and believe God has a better plan B, or we can get mad, depressed, or discouraged as we wallow in self-pity. I guarantee that the self-pity route will free you up from experiencing the joy of God's plan B, C, or D. Self-pity also does a great job of making all your loved ones miserable too!

Plan A didn't work out for me, so I chose to enjoy the opportunity of hanging out with my wife, while serving my son and friend. By the way, it turned out to be a blast! Then after all the early adversity, God's plan C turned out to be one of my most memorable hunts ever.

Trust the process. God has something better for you no matter what the devil may throw at you. God is always three steps ahead. God has a great plan for your life. The bad choices of your own or others or the devil's attacks will not keep God from preparing alternative plans for your life. He will always have a plan B, C, or F or even Z. He is always at least three chess moves ahead, you can always trust him.

For I know the plans that I have for you, declares the Lord, plans for welfare and not for calamity to give you a future and a hope. Then you will call upon Me and come and pray to Me, and I will listen to you. You will seek Me and find me when you search for Me with all your heart. (Jeremiah 29:11–13)

Don't fret. Just trust him today!

CHAPTER 11

The Fall

The fear of heights is reportedly one of the top three fears in all of North America. It follows only death and public speaking on the survey. Fear and respect are similar but significantly different. Fear often prevents us from even trying something, while a healthy respect of something means we simply apply caution while we attempt it.

Let's be honest—if you have ever fallen a significant distance, you're aware of the rush and feeling of freedom as you rapidly descend. That adrenaline rush can be very exhilarating. It's that abrupt stop that hurts. I've personally had many such exhilarating experiences. The worst was a twenty-foot fall off a barn roof. Luckily there was a nice concrete slab at the bottom to break my fall! My guardian angels must have called in reinforcements that day. I landed on my feet and then rolled to a stop. Miraculously, I did not break or sprain a thing. PTL! But every joint in my body ached for about a week. I can only guess that's what it feels like to get hit by a truck.

I've also had numerous tree stand incidents over the years. I've had screw-in tree stand steps pull out on me, and branches have broken. My climbing stand has slid down several trees with me still attached.

I personally know guys who have had their backs broken and dislocated their knees and shoulders from falls. One guy got his wedding ring caught on a screw-in step, and when his foot slipped, he all but ripped his finger off. Another friend had his foot somehow wedged between his climber and the tree. After trying unsuccessfully to free himself, he fell backward, where he hung upside down. He hung there for several long hours in cold temperatures before he was finally found and rescued by his wife.

Let's face it—gravity is nothing to be trifled with, and it will always win. But we should not fear it. Just treat it with respect and caution while keeping in mind that nobody is bulletproof. No matter how tough you are, or think you are, you really aren't. Just watch any NFL football game and you'll see guys a lot tougher, stronger, and in better shape than you are getting carted off the field after a violent hit—a hit a lot less violent than a tree stand fall. Gravity will move us a lot faster than any linebacker can run. And I'm pretty certain that very few of us actually wear a helmet and pads into their tree stands.

The worst fall I was ever witness to happened about twenty years ago. I was visiting a friend in northern Wisconsin. The rut was on, and the bucks were moving. Dick was a meat hunter, but like most of us, he dreamed of big bucks. Dick lived on the border of Wisconsin and Michigan's upper peninsula. He would buy deer tags for both states to make sure he had a full freezer by the season's end.

The most common hunting method for meat hunters in the north woods is to sit over a corn pile. This method is legal, but it gives no guarantees that you will even see a deer, let alone get a shot at one. I mentioned in a previous chapter that this country is big. There are tens of thousands of acres of woods and swamps with no grain fields or oaks to sit over or in. You can hunt for weeks over game trails without ever seeing a deer. Most of the locals go with the corn pile method. Corn attracts does, and does attract bucks. And the sight of a buck will get your adrenaline flowing no matter what your choice of hunting method may be.

Dick invited me to hunt with him that afternoon in Michigan. Since I did not have a Michigan hunting license, I left my bow at the house and tagged along with my trusty rattling horns. Dick had never tried calling deer before, and after I shared some of the stories of the deer I had called in, he was super excited to experience it for himself.

That afternoon was almost perfectly calm. The cool temps were in the mid-twenties, and there was about a foot of fresh snow on the ground. The skies were overcast with some light lake effect snow drifting down.

Dick would climb into his stand overlooking the bait while I would rattle off the ground. I would be downwind, about forty yards from the bait. I was situated on the edge of a ridge, with a swampy, pothole lake below me. This would allow my scent to drift out over the lake, hopefully preventing me from getting winded. It was a great setup. The forest was a mixture of young and mature evergreens. Dick's stand was over twenty feet high, in a huge, old white pine tree. He had been hunting from that stand for many years and felt safe in it. The metal stand was securely chained to the tree.

I was just finishing up my makeshift ground blind as Dick ascended to his perch. As I watched him reach his summit, the last branch he was stepping on suddenly broke. I watched in horror as a seventy-year-old man rag-dolled down that white pine tree. Dick bounced off several of the branches before he landed spread eagle on his back. With my heart in my throat, I cleared those forty yards at NFL combine speed.

"Are you all right?" I asked, fearing the worst.

Slowly Dick opened his eyes. He wiggled his fingers and then flexed his arms. Then to my shock and delight, he sat up and said, "Boy, that's never happened before!"

Dick then grunted, rolled over, and climbed back up to his perch for the evening hunt. Crazy? Maybe. But it was the rut, and our time was short. Later after dark, as we hiked back to the truck, Dick sternly warned me not to tell his wife about his fall. He feared she wouldn't let him finish out the bow season.

By the time supper was over, Dick spilled the beans and confessed the whole story to his wife. Apparently the pain from his broken ribs was too much to hide. All things considered, Dick really got off easy. Broken ribs heal, and a shortened season can still leave us dreaming about next year, while broken backs, necks, or even death usually accompany such falls.

So what should we do? Stop hunting? Maybe we should stop pursuing all adrenaline-pumping adventures for fear of a low-percentage consequence. Maybe we should just all sit on the couch and watch TV. We can play it safe as we live vicariously through others as we squander our few precious years.

Not in my world! I suggest that we continue to enjoy our favorite pastimes while simply proceeding with caution. As for me, I still use tree stands—although I admit, steel ladder stands have long since replaced the pallets I used to nail in the branches forty years ago.

I find that ladder stands are by far the easiest to put up and the safest stands available. I also religiously wear a safety harness to lessen my chances of a fall. I still hunt in areas that contain healthy wolf, grizzly, and rattlesnake populations. Again, we just need to proceed with caution.

A righteous man falls seven times and rises again. (Proverbs 24:16)

Dick climbed right back up that tree. I have reroofed dozens of buildings since my exhilarating barn incident. What is God asking you to do that fear is preventing you from doing? Fear is one of Satan's most powerful weapons. It's a head game that paralyzes its victims by planting simple perceptions of worst-case scenarios into our heads. Then we buy into his game by focusing on them. The more we dwell or focus on the what ifs, the more paralyzed by fear we become. Fear then robs our lives from the joys and ministries God had intended for us to be a part of. It's no wonder the most common phrase in the Bible is, "Do not fear!" A righteous man lives by faith and is characterized by his boldness.

For God has not given us a spirit of timidity, but of power and love and discipline. (2 Timothy 1:7)

My challenge for you today is to use his bold, powerful spirit to empower you to do whatever God has put in your heart to do. Live your life to its fullest, both spiritually and physically. When your life is over, both God in heaven and man on earth should be able to say, "Well done, good and faithful servant. He lived his life to its fullest, with no regrets. He went out with his boots on."

Tim McGraw has a great song entitled "Live like you were dying" it is a very inspirational song that reminds us that our time here is short and we should live a fearless life with no regrets.

After all, living and existing are not the same thing. God bless you with a fearless life today!

CHAPTER 12

Dave's Bull

I don't think I've ever met anyone who didn't have a bucket list—you know, the mental dream list of things you want to see, experience, or accomplish before your time on earth is up. It seems that a lot of elderly folks I know try to play catch-up with their lists well into their seventies and eighties.

Two of my mom's bucket list items she successfully checked off were helicopter rides in Alaska and doing aerobatics in a WWI biplane. Another young at heart lady, named Phyllis, would check off one bucket list item a year on her birthday. They included hot air balloon rides and skydiving. Did I mention she was in her eighties? It was truly a privilege for me to have known these women.

In the last chapter, I spoke of living out our lives with no regrets or to "live like you were dying" these old gals attempted to do just that. I believe it would be almost impossible to do everything we have ever dreamed of, but somethings are definitely attainable.

My buddy Dave is only in his fifties but dreamed of hunting and harvesting a bull elk. I jokingly reminded him that every year those mountains get a little higher, so he might not want to wait too long. Bull elk are certainly an attainable goal, especially if you have the money. Many high-end outfitters boast of 90 to 100 percent success rates. But most of us have families to feed and struggle to scrape together enough shekels just for the exorbitant cost of a nonresident elk tag, let alone pay a high-end outfitter. Dave and I both fall into that category.

We could be considered the original public land, do-it-yourself hunters. Many of the public lands I've been blessed to hunt boast success rates of 6 to 10 percent. But hey, with odds like that, sign me up! That's way better than the lottery.

A few years back, Dave and I were planning a backcountry Colorado elk hunt with a mutual acquaintance who used to be a guide in Colorado. This was to be our dream hunt. But like most dreams, they are not without a little darkness, snoring, and the occasional jab from your spouse. In this dream, the jerking and twitching started about the middle of August. That's when our mutual acquaintance backed out and left us with nothing but sweaty sheets. It was then time for plan B to be implemented.

I first reassured Dave that we would still be elk hunting that fall. I then suggested maybe we bowhunt rather than using our rifles and fighting all the crowds. Dave was all for it. After a few phone calls, plan B was in place. Our new destination was now Marble, Colorado. It would be our new home for the first week or so of September. A friend of mine even allowed us the use of his cabin there. I love it when a plan comes together.

Accompanying us on our trip was my son Mark, a high school senior at the time, and Trevor. Trevor was an enthusiastic young bowhunter. As a sophomore soccer player, he assured me that he was up to the task. Trevor had lost his dad to a motorcycle accident a few years earlier, and we felt led to include him in on this adventure.

I tried to keep expectations realistic throughout the planning stages and the long drive to Colorado. I received reinforcements when we arrived at the ranger station. We told the ranger we needed maps of the area for our elk hunt. The perplexed look on her face was accompanied by her statement, "Elk hunt? That's sheep country!" Hmm, sheep county? It's a good thing Trever was a soccer player.

Sheep country was right. The mountains were steep and high. Much of our time was spent in a three-point stance with one hand on the ground. I would later take pictures of planes flying hundreds of feet below us. We were all in awe as we drove up to Dan's beautiful cabin. It was located halfway up a steep, rocky face.

As the guys unloaded our gear, I hiked up the road to a game trail Dan had told me about. We would need to follow this trail up to the area we planned to hunt the next morning. As I hiked up the trail, attempting to get a daylight lay of the land, I noticed a large pile of fresh bear scat. Lying next to the scat was an old tennis shoe. I could hardly wait to get back and tell the guys. During our drive to Colorado, Trevor was very verbal about his, ahh, we'll say bear apprehensions.

The guys thought I was just joking about the scat and shoe until five o'clock the next morning when their flashlights illuminated the scene. You could have cut the tension in the air with a knife, as I enjoyed a good laugh about it. About an hour later, just after daylight, I was surprised to see a nice black bear run down the mountain parallel to us. He stopped about thirty yards away, for just long enough for me to practice drawing on him. Trevor stayed remarkably close to me the rest of the day.

The next couple of days were spent canvassing different areas trying to locate some elk, with no luck at all. The weather forecast had called for a 30 percent chance of rain each day. We quickly discovered that meant it would rain 30 percent of the time. Without fail, every morning it would rain until about nine or ten o'clock. This rain-soaked vegetation left us soaked to the bone.

On the third day we finally located some wallows and other encouraging elk sign. But with the high altitudes, rain, cold temperatures, and sweaty climbs, it didn't take long before Trevor came down with hypothermia. With Dave and Trevor both battling altitude sickness and Trevor's hypothermia, we didn't need Dr. Oz to tell us to head back to the cabin and leave that area for another day.

The next day we left Trevor and Dave resting at the cabin while Mark and I scouted out a new area. As daylight began to cut through the aspens, I let out a bugle and received an immediate response. Our hearts skipped a beat as this was the first response of the trip. The six-mile hike in was now well worth every step. We actually located three decent bulls that morning. But try as we might, Mark and I were unable to close the deal, mostly due to the shifting mountain winds. But we were overjoyed that we had finally found elk! On our hike out, we were all smiles as we were eager to share the news with Dave and Trevor. Tomorrow would certainly be the day.

Four o'clock in the morning came pretty early as we ate a quick breakfast and started out on the long six-mile trek up the mountain. Our anticipation was running high as we followed an old horse trail over creeks and through dew-drenched meadows. We were often surrounded by stands of golden aspens, making the long hike in absolutely beautiful.

Our first setup was a bust. Nothing showed up or responded to my calls. But our second setup brought our blood pressure up. I worked in a nice five-point bull but couldn't seem to get him closer than seventy yards. Apparently he didn't like the young man in the black T-shirt crawling around in the aspens just behind me. Hmmm, go figure.

After we regrouped, Dave informed me that a really nice six-by-six also came in silently behind me, but he retreated without making a sound after catching our scent. As frustrating as elk hunting can be, I live for those encounters.

The four of us then followed a distant bugle as we headed further up the trail to the edge of a meadow. The meadow was in a deep valley and transitioned into a willow thicket. Aspens lined both side walls of the canyon as a creek trickled down the middle. The four of us must have sounded like a bulldozer going through that thick brush as we noisily closed the distance. I assured the guys not to worry because that's what an angry bull would sound like.

We had two bulls bugling at us from across the willow-choked valley. They were both slightly up the adjacent mountain slope. After a half hour, I watched the bigger bull take his harem further up the mountain away from us. But the solo bull bugled back and forth with me for over two hours.

We had spread out along the edge of the willows in hopes that one of us would get a shot. As I raked a tree with a branch, I would mix in cow and calf calls. I would also sporadically bugle. Every time he would seem to lose interest, I would mix it up or move to try to entice him over our way. I could see him occasionally as he zigzagged back and forth across the creek. He would often stop and rake the willows with his six-by-six rack. After two and a half hours of cat and mouse, the bull finally committed and stepped from the willows. The bull offered Dave a twenty-yard shot, which he gladly took. Dave's arrow hitting the bull just behind the front shoulder. The bull wheeled at the shot and crashed off back into the thick willows.

High-fives and excitement ensued as we waited to take up the trail. After a thirty-minute wait, we began trailing him, only to quickly jump the bull in the thick willows. After backing out, we decided it was best to wait a few hours before picking up the trail again.

While we ate our lunch, the weather changed on a dime. The mild seventy-degree temps suddenly dropped to the mid-thirties. It started to hail viciously, turning the ground white with pea-sized ice balls. Minutes later the sky erupted into a heavy downpour. Cold and wet, we began to pursue what was left of the blood trail, only to quickly jump the bull again. Both of his beds were less than fifty yards apart. We prayed about our best options and decided to give him a few more hours.

This time, I sent Dave and Mark around the willow-choked bottom to the other side of the valley. My hope was if the bull was still alive, the guys could cut off his escape route. Meanwhile, Trevor and I would take up the trail or grid search the willows for the bull. The rain was intense as we waded through the willows. The bull's trail quickly vanished in the rain, and to my surprise, so did Trevor.

I spent the next two hours searching for Trevor, calling out frantically for him. I couldn't believe I was now searching the thick tangle of willows for a fifteen-year-old as well as the bull. I finally reached into my pocket to radio Dave and found the radio was actually floating in my pocket. It was five o'clock when my prayers were answered and I found Trevor. Thank you, Lord! As a sheriff's chaplain, I've had the miserable task of telling a worried mother that their teen wasn't coming home. That's something I never want to experience again!

We were wet, hungry, tired, and emotionally exhausted as we made our way up the ridge to find Dave. "I'm sorry, Dave, but we lost the trail. We are going to have to find Mark and head out before dark and hypothermia comes calling again."

It was like deja vu as we walked and called looking for Mark. He wasn't where I expected him to be. We were yelling and whistling as we spread out along the ridge searching for him. Here we go again! My sense of humor had taken the last flight home about six hours earlier. I was both frustrated and worried.

Finally, after we again regrouped, we walked into a meadow filled with chest-high grass and shrubs, that is when I spotted an orange hat hanging high in a tree. PTL! Mark was right below it. When he saw us, he began running toward us, bouncing along as he hollered, "I got the bull! I got the bull! I got the bull!" Then, wham! He stepped in a hole and face-planted right in front of us. Thanks, Mark, I needed that!

I laughed so hard I practically cried. Hundreds of emotions welled up inside of us all as Mark told us his tale. As Mark moved to his cutoff point, he found the mortally wounded bull already lying on the ridge. Mark then made a perfect heart shot on the bull. The bull proceeded to get up and run thirty more yards before wobbling to a stop. Mark's second shot probably wasn't necessary, but it dropped the bull in his tracks. Dave's initial shot was mortal but had hit the bull at an odd angle and a little further back than we had first thought, taking the bull through one lung and the liver.

The rain had finally stopped as we snapped pictures and retold our experiences. The guys worked diligently to cut up the elk. Meanwhile, I built a fire that served to warm and dry the guys out.

The roasted elk meat I cooked over that fire was by far one of the best meals any us had ever enjoyed. I didn't say best tasting, just the most enjoyable! That hot protein would have to sustain us for at least another seven hours.

With the majority of the elk hanging safely in a tree. Mark placed the bull's head on his shoulders as I loaded up my pack frame with delicious elk meat. It was just getting dark as we started the six-mile hike down the mountain. We weren't out of the woods yet as Dave and Trevor had battled altitude sickness off and on all week long. Dave's knee had also given out on him repeatedly. Many more trials were awaiting us on the trip back down the mountain.

Despite all the trials we encountered that day, words really can't describe the joy we shared as we rested in a starlit meadow that night. The memory of us looking up at the beautiful star-studded sky, surrounded by friends as we enjoyed the sweet taste of success, will never be forgotten. We finally got off the mountain about two o'clock that morning totally exhausted. It had been twenty-two long, hard hours since our adventure had begun that morning.

There were some extreme highs and lows that we experienced that day, but the highs and lows are truly indicative of a bucket list item. Life itself, if truly lived, is full of highs and lows. Valleys seem to follow most Rocky mountain high experiences. The possible loss of people we care about can make even harvesting a six-by-six bull seem trivial. I lost and found Trevor and Mark that day, which is kind of funny considering Mark didn't even know he was lost. He was just anxiously waiting for us with the ultimate prize of Dave's hard-earned trophy.

As you go through life's highs and lows, remember, this is your journey. You can't control the weather or people's actions or many of the other situations we find ourselves in. You can only control your response to these situations. We sometimes need to be reminded that God cares for your lost loved ones even more than you do. He cares about what you are going through. Remember that the harder the battle you face, the greater your victory story will be.

On this hunt, we were all eventually reunited to share in the prize. In life, Jesus promised us that all who put their faith in him will be reunited with him someday in glory. This reuniting will also include all the others who put their faith in him. Those believers will all share the prize of an eternity in heaven with the Lord. I look forward to that day of being reunited with the Lord as well as with my loved ones. I can hardly wait to see them joyfully bouncing through a meadow toward me—hopefully this time without the face-plant!

Enjoy your highs and lows. Lows usually end with a high, so don't give up! God has a great ending planned for your story. But you have to hang in there because your prize bull may be just on the other side of the valley.

CHAPTER 13

The Waterhole

TV, radio, the Internet, and even YouTube all make their money by advertising. Many people will tune into the Super Bowl just to watch the commercials. Some of these products have been around forever while others introduce us to new products that we are told we can't live without.

I'm really not much of a gadget guy. I shoot my recurves and longbows with bare fingers. I shoot my compounds with the same strap-on index finger release I've had for twenty-plus years. Both my fingers and my release have served me well over the years.

But the problem is that I have struggled with target panic off and on for over thirty years. Target panic can come in a variety of forms, from punching the trigger to freezing off the target to jerking or flinching. It's a mental problem that can be a nightmare for archers.

I've read many articles on how to cure target panic. One thing that is supposed to help is to switch from a finger trigger release to a thumb trigger release. So when the local archery shop was having a big sale, yours truly, rushed out and broke the bank on a new thumb release. Boy, I couldn't wait to try it out.

I lived across the street from the church I pastored, so I took advantage of my position by setting up my own archery range in our church gym. I could shoot out to thirty yards in the gym and up to sixty yards if I shot down the hall into the gym. PTL! I have never had a casualty. Who says prayer doesn't work?

My first few shots with the new release felt really awkward to say the least. But as I settled in, I began to feel more and more comfortable using my thumb to squeeze the trigger. After a dozen or so shots, I was able to start focusing more on my form than on the mechanics of the thumb release. Draw back, anchor, settle the pin on the target, breathe, release. And boy did it release!

I let go of my release and watched in horror as it flew through my bow and slammed into the brick gym wall above my target. Talk about an adrenaline rush! Although pretty banged up, it appeared to still work. With my heart in my throat, I proceeded to stuff that evil thing back into my bow case, where it would stay for several years. Back to the safety of my strap on finger release I went. Well, there went a hundred bucks down the tube!

Fast forward a couple of years. I was now shooting with a friend on his backyard range. He had switched from a finger to a thumb-style release and was praising its benefits. As I shared my gym experience, he laughed and then shared his. His first experience with a thumb release didn't go nearly as well as mine did. When he let go of his release, it smashed into his bow hand, shattering several bones. His smashed hand required extensive surgery to repair the damage done by his release. Think about it—a hunk of metal flying at three hundred feet per second contacting your unprotected hand. Ouch! That could make the most pious cuss like a sailor.

"So why on earth are you still shooting the thumb release?" I asked.

"Well, you get used to it," he said. "And just look at my tight groups!" Hey, nobody ever accused him of being the sharpest crayon in the box.

Well I guess I'm not either, because the week before I left for my Montana elk hunt, he talked me into using that dreaded thumb release again.

The following week I met up with Jim and his son Kent in the Missouri breaks. Hunting had been incredibly slow for them. They had been hunting hard for about ten days before I had gotten there, and Jim had yet to set his eyes on an elk. But new guys often bring new optimism, enthusiasm, as well as new ideas. Within two days we had all seen elk, but it was now time for Kent to head back home.

I suggested to Jim that we go and try a certain water hole we all knew of. Jim informed me that Kent had already checked it out and there was no elk sign to be found. Elk are very different from whitetails. Whitetails have a home range of about a mile and a half, while elk have no limits to their home range. Elk tend to follow the same daily routines until they are pressured. Then they may relocate five or even ten miles away. As long as food and water are available, elk are just as content on the prairie as they are on a dark-timbered mountain slope.

Jim reluctantly tagged along as we rechecked the water hole. Depending upon the year, this pond could be as dry as a bone, but this year it was full of water. But more importantly, since Kent had checked it last, the elk had now moved in. It was now steaming with fresh elk sign.

We quickly set up a decoy near the water's edge directly in front of Jim's makeshift blind. I set up across the pond from him about sixty yards away. My blind consisted of a three-legged stool that I leveled in behind a sage bush halfway up the dike. The wind was blowing from Jim across the pond toward me. Our scent would then travel up and over the dike down into a steep ravine.

As evening settled in, my calls enticed a nice five-point bull and a cow to come down for a closer look. They really wanted a drink, but they did not like the decoy. They eventually wandered off without giving either of us any shot opportunities. Later on, a lone spike also came in, but he didn't like the decoy either. He was kind enough to offer both of us shots, but he really wasn't the kind of bull you come to the breaks for.

The next night was similar to the first, only we left the decoy at home. We saw and heard elk but didn't get any shot opportunities. On the third night on the pond, we again decided to adjust our strategy. We left the decoy at home, but this time I would only call if we thought it was absolutely necessary.

As we approached the pond, I could not believe my eyes. There, lying about ten yards off the water's edge among the driftwood, was a five-point elk shed! How I or Kent or any of the countless other hunters had not seen it was beyond me. Was it a sign from above? Surely tonight would be the night. Thank you, Lord!

Things started off slow that night, with no animal sightings and no bugling bulls to be heard, just the constant drone of mosquitoes and an occasional magpie. About a half hour before dark, I let out a bugle and received an immediate response. I was surprised when the bull started screaming at me as he headed in our direction. He was coming in fast as he headed down the hill from behind Jim.

It was nearing the end of our hunt, and we had decided to shoot a cow if one presented itself. This bull was preceded by five cows. I knew Jim wouldn't be able to see the animals until they were literally right in front of him. I prayed he wouldn't shoot one of those cows. The bull was in the rear of the group and was without a doubt the biggest five-point I had ever seen. He was much larger than most six points. He was very tall and had incredibly long points.

Jim's adrenaline was really flowing as a cow stopped and started drinking fifteen yards below him. She was nervous and knew something wasn't quite right. When she spooked, she took the rest of her peers with her. The whole herd started trotting along the opposite side of the pond parallel to Jim. Jim took a shot as the bull passed by him at twenty-five yards. His hurried shot flew low as the bull trotted along.

At the time, I wasn't sure if Jim had hit the bull or not, so I was at full draw when the herd stopped to look back. My fifty-yard sight pin settled on the bull's heart. Twang! My shot was on its way.

I watched as my arrow flew perfectly toward its mark, only to drop just below his heart. I later rearranged his location at fifty-six yards. An arrow can drop a lot between fifty and fifty-six yards. The herd trotted up the hill and then started feeding in a ravine about a hundred yards opposite us.

In the meantime, a nice six-point, or six-by-six for you easterners, had crossed the trail behind Jim and was watching the show. He was slowly working his way around us before he eventually disappeared off to my left.

Then a cow and a different five-point bull came down from the west, or to my left. I could not believe this action. They walked up and over the end of my dike. The cow stopped on the dike, about twenty yards away, staring in my direction. While she stared, the bull went down to get a drink. He stopped quartering away at thirty-five yards. I came to full draw, but I could see my arrow wouldn't clear the brush. I slowly raised myself up from my seated position, still at full draw. When I felt I could clear the brush, I let my shot go. I watched in disbelief as my arrow failed to clear some of the sagebrush and deflected into the ground. The bull wheeled around and trotted up the dike.

He only went about ten yards when he stopped, totally perplexed. He wanted that water and was clueless as to what had just happened. His girlfriend had trotted off, and he was torn between following her and getting a drink. While he pondered his choices, I nocked my third arrow. The bull made his decision and walked about five yards closer to the water as I came to full draw.

Don't screw this up! Is there enough arrow clearance? Check, shot angle? Check, range? Thirty yards! Pick a spot? Check, breathe, release! To my horror, I watched in slow motion as my thumb release sailed through my bow and over the bull's back, landing in the water several yards behind him. My arrow had only traveled a short distance before skidding to a stop, ten yards from my makeshift blind.

The bull? Well, he and his lady friend headed west at warp speed. I can laugh now, but I wanted to cry at the time. Seriously, three shots in what? Ten minutes? And you throw your release at him? Bonehead! I had one arrow left, and PTL! I also had packed my old, faithful finger release in my fanny pack. A minute later I was again locked and loaded.

The sun was down, but in those last few minutes of fading shooting light, I looked to the west to enjoy the sunset. The breathtaking sunset was only enhanced by the sight of a beautiful six-by-six bull, sky-lined on the top of the ridge! The magnificent colors contrasting his dark silhouette will be forever engraved in my mind.

I could not believe this was happening. After a few minutes he cautiously worked his way down the trail and stopped broadside at thirty yards. I was at full draw and again went through my mental checklist. Anchor, pick a spot, relax, breathe, squeeze the trigger. The bull jumped and ran at the shot. He stopped and looked back at about seventy yards. It was almost like he was saying, "The rumors are true. You can't hit the broadside of a bull!"

The next morning we returned and recovered all five of our arrows. And yes, I did wade out in that muddy, cold water to retrieve that cursed thumb release. It is for sale if anyone is interested.

Later, back at the cabin, I decided to take some practice shots. My first practice shot at fifteen yards completely missed the target. Hmm. Apparently an aluminum thumb release traveling at three hundred feet per second when contacting a site bracket will adversely affect the site pins location! Who'd a thunk it?

So what can we learn from my epic failures? Number one, never switch equipment a week before a hunt. Number two, thumb releases are the spawn of hell. Number three, never give up until you're out of arrows. Then get more arrows!

Spiritually, we need to listen to that still, small voice. Believers are equipped with the indwelling presence of the Holy Spirit. He will speak to us if we are willing to listen. He will lead us in the way we should go, as well as warning us of dangers that lay ahead. Jesus referred to the Holy Spirit as our comforter, helper, and teacher and the promise of the father. Jesus told his followers that it was to their advantage that he go away so the Father could send the Holy Spirit. When Jesus was on the earth, he was limited to only one place at one time. The Holy Spirit indwells all those who believe for all time. If you have questions about these promises, please read John 14–16.

The Holy Spirit warned me repeatedly not to hunt with that thumb release. There was always a check in my spirit, even when I was buying it. I ignored his warnings in exchange for slightly improved accuracy. My ignoring him cost me two really nice bulls. It could have cost me much more in the way of a smashed hand or wrist.

We've all been tempted to do something while a nagging little voice says, "No! Don't do it!" Learn to listen to that voice and learn from your mistakes. God really does have your best interests in mind. You will do well to listen to him.

I had to leave the next day, but Jim? Well, after three weeks of hard hunting, he heeded my final advice, and two days later he harvested that same six-point bull. He was sitting in my ground blind about four miles away. The Spirit will often speak through people too. Just remember that the Holy Spirit will never contradict his written word.

Are you listening to him?

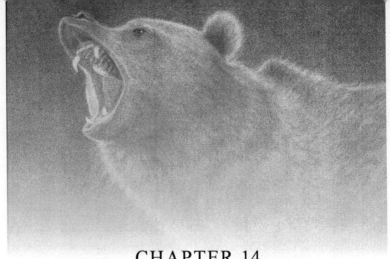

CHAPTER 14

Grandpa's Bear

A quick glance around any kid's bedroom, will tell you a lot about him or her—the child's likes or dislikes, interests, and accomplishments. Children's rooms will often display their hopes, dreams, and aspirations. Adults are not much different, unless, of course, you're married. Then it's often a game of compromise. Compromising means fish and game trophies are often relegated to our garages, basements, and/or attics. Apparently a ten-point buck mount doesn't match the floral wallpaper. Which makes no sense at all when you consider educated people tend to group them as flora and fauna. Sorry, I digress.

As a child, my bedroom said a lot about me. While my friends displayed posters of Darth Vader and Farrah Fawcett, I had a large six-by-six elk rack on one wall and a huge grizzly bear rug on the other. The bearskin hung proudly on the wall alongside my bed. My morning and evening routines often included running my fingers through his thick fur coat. I loved to admire his enormous head, teeth, and claws. They were truly awe inspiring. Sorry, Vader, but when it comes to truly being a bad character, you've got nothing on a silvertip grizzly!

Originally a Montana resident, the great bear came to reside in Wisconsin through my grandpa George. Grandpa worked as an engineer with the Milwaukee Road railroad. In his spare time, Grandpa loved to hunt and fish. He had taken several trips out west to hunt elk and mule deer, while his Canada hunts produced at least one big bull moose.

I can't remember ever missing an opening day of trout season with Grandpa. Without fail, the first Saturday of May Grandpa would pick me up bright and early, and we were off to slay whatever eight-inch brooky, rainbow, or brown the DNR happened to stock that year. We usually did quite well, providing I had done my part in ridding the local golf course of those pesky nightcrawlers. Nightcrawlers were also known as angle bugs, as Grandpa would call them. Expensive fly rods and Cabela's waders would not be found in Grandpa's trunk. No, it was angle bugs and level-wind reels. These were the poor man's weapons of choice, but they worked just fine.

It was on such a fishing adventure, complete with our high-tech gear, that I asked Grandpa to share the story of his great bear hunt. We were sitting on a railroad trestle with our braided lines dangling in the trout stream. As we sat back and enjoyed the sack lunches Grandma had prepared for us, Grandpa began by relaying the story of his Montana elk hunt. I will retell it here to the best of my recollection.

It was the 1930s, and Grandpa's old 30-06 had brought down an elk just before dark. He and his guide had field dressed the animal but decided to wait until the next morning to finish packing him out. It turns out that decision would cost Grandpa a lot of meat!

When they arrived the next morning to retrieve the animal, they discovered a grizzly had cleaned up the gut pile and one of the quarters. The guide told Grandpa that it was a big bear and then asked him if he wanted to take a crack at the great bear. After all of a microsecond of prayerful consideration, Grandpa acknowledged he was all in.

Knowing the bear would return to finish feeding on the elk, they quickly built a little scaffold or tree stand in the crotch of a tree a whopping eight feet off the ground. The game plan was for Grandpa to spend the night curled up in his sleeping bag, precariously balancing on the scaffolding while he waited for the big bear to return for his evening snack. That meant spending the night alone in the dark, waiting for a huge hungry grizzly, with only his adrenaline to keep him awake. We must also keep in mind that hunting regulations for bears in the 1930s were close to nonexistent.

It was about one or two o'clock in the morning when Grandpa could finally hear the bear coming up from the draw. Anyone who has ever hunted black bears knows that even a big boar can ghost in and out of a bait on dry leaves without hardly making a sound. But this old boy was keeping no secrets as he approached the elk carcass. He was snapping off trees and letting anything and everything in the vicinity know that he was coming and it was his elk.

In the full moonlight, Grandpa could clearly see the bear's enormous silhouette. Grandpa patiently waited for the big bear to turn broadside. As Grandpa squeezed the trigger, his .30-06 lit up the night sky with a blinding flash. The bear wheeled around, snapping at his side before standing on his hind legs. The enraged bear noticed Grandpa chambering another round. Grandpa's heart must have been working overtime! He was sitting in a tree only eight feet off the ground, while a ten-foot grizzly bear was staring him in the eyes! Grandpa's second shot hit the bear in the neck and sent him on a bulldozing death run back down the draw.

The minutes must have felt like hours as they slowly ticked by. Grandpa's thoughts must have been racing as he waited patiently for the guide to return in the morning. There would be no sleep that night! Imagine waiting alone in the dark, knowing a monstrous wounded grizzly was somewhere out in the shadows.

When the guide finally showed up, well after daylight, they trailed and quickly recovered the king of the mountain within a few hundred yards. People often overestimate the size of both black and grizzly bears. It's just human nature to think the big, shaggy beasts are bigger than they actually are, especially if you're not accustomed to seeing these awesome creatures.

The adjectives I used to describe this bear are huge, monstrous, and enormous, and they are not in any shape or form exaggerations. To date, this bear ranks as the largest silvertip grizzly ever taken in the lower forty-eight states.

Ironically, for close to forty years, Grandpa's world-class trophy was relegated by Grandma to a closet in their attic. It still amazes me how a 110-pound woman can make a 200-pound man back down quicker than 1,000-pound grizzly!

It was some time in the mid-1970s that I was finally able to talk both my grandpa and my parents into letting us keep the bear at our house, where it could be properly and proudly displayed.

Sadly, over the years several different dogs had taken a real disdain to that bear. Their hatred resulted in unprovoked, vicious attacks, which left the prize rug in a less than pristine condition. In later years, after more one-sided battles and for the love of some scared little girls, his remains were finally discarded. Personally, I would have loved to have had the chance at salvaging the head and claws, but what's gone is gone. Dwelling upon what is lost will only steal your joy.

Grandpa's bear is a stark reminder that no matter how praiseworthy a trophy may be or how it may be valued here on earth, all of our trophies will someday end up in either the trash or a garage sale.

Do not store up for yourselves treasures on earth, where moth and rust destroy, and where thieves break in and steal. But store up for yourselves treasures in heaven, where neither moth nor rust destroys, and where thieves do not break in and steal; for where your treasure is, there your heart will be also. (Matthew 6:19–21)

Those verses are Jesus's way of reminding us that nobody's hearse will be pulling a U-Haul trailer. What truly matters is first our relationship with Jesus. Next is our relationship with mankind. Everything else is secondary. Those heavenly treasures are the fruit that comes with a right relationship with the Lord. As we walk with him, we can accomplish the tasks that he prepared for us to do. Scripture also says that without faith, it is impossible to please him.

If we stop and think about what we won't have in heaven, we can then refocus on obtaining what we will have in heaven, and it all starts with faith.

CHAPTER 15

Pete

It was about noon as we slowly and deliberately trudged down the mountain trail in the rain. We were totally exhausted, soaked to the bone, dejected, and I was angrily questioning why I was even there. After a week of hard hunting, we had yet to even spot an elk. Tomorrow was our last day, and we would have to call it quits by noon. We had hiked fifteen to twenty miles a day that week, climbing new mountains every day as we desperately attempted to locate fresh elk sign without any kind of luck. I'm usually a very optimistic kind of guy, but on that day, it had finally gotten to me. To make matters worse, I never really wanted to be there in the first place.

Earlier that spring, I had applied for, but didn't receive, the special draw unit I desired. That meant I had to either hunt the western general units or sell back my tag at a 20 percent loss. I never felt at peace about it either way. With the sell-back deadline quickly approaching, I earnestly prayed for direction, asking the Lord, "What should I do?"

After checking out some different options, I decided to keep my elk tag. I settled on giving the beautiful Swan Valley in western

Montana a try. After speaking with my sons-in-laws, I was offered a place to stay, along with some direction on where to hunt. They also warned me I should not hunt alone. The Swan Valley boasts some of the highest grizzly numbers in the United States. I was also informed the wolves had decimated the local elk herds, so I should not expect much in the way of elk activity.

Wow! No elk, but lots of wolves and grizzly bears. It all sounded almost too good to be true. I had never hunted the western part of the state before and figured I'd give it a try.

The in-laws also informed me that I shouldn't expect to encounter small bands of elk in each drainage. They said instead, the elk were now grouped up into large herds. The larger herds offered the elk some protection from the thriving wolf population. This hunt would really be feast or famine. I was also told to expect mile after mile of empty pursuits. But hopefully, I'd eventually find the larger herds.

To help explain how bad the wolf population had gotten, the Fish and Game Department's December "pre-winter" elk count revealed only nine calves per hundred cows. That, my friends, is seriously a herd in decline! As my favorite bumper sticker says, "Save a hound! Smoke a pack today!"

All I needed now was a partner—someone who would be willing to tag along just for the experience and of course to help me be bear aware! If my partner wanted to hunt, his only choice in over-the-counter hunting tags were for wolves. Luckily wolf tags are cheap and plentiful. I believe at that time a nonresident could get multiple wolf tags for under a hundred bucks.

As I prayed about who might accompany me, the Lord brought to mind my old roommate and best man, Pete. I hadn't seen Pete in a while, so I gave him a call. God's timing is always perfect. After I explained my dilemma, it took Pete less than ten seconds to jump on the opportunity. It seems life had not been kind to Pete, and he was really going through a rough patch. My call and this hunt, for that matter, could not have come at a better time for him. As for me? Well, it meant the hunt was on!

As I splashed down the fire trail that day, my frustrations mounted. The devil used my current circumstances to remind me of many unsuccessful hunts of the past. My mind raced back to so many close calls and failed attempts. My past attempts were plagued with many empty freezers and elk tag soup. I'm not a whiner, but I sure felt like one that day. I was wallowing in self-pity.

A big-branch antler bull had been my heart's desire ever since I was six. Now over forty years later, my heart's desire had still somehow eluded me. I had successfully called in many bulls for friends and family. But when was it going to be my turn? Whine, wallow! Why was I limited to only close calls? Whine, wallow! I just couldn't seem to close the deal on a dream bull. Whine, wallow! Have you ever been there?

As my mind wallowed in self-pity, my thoughts raced back to a similar week I had in the Missouri breaks. It had also been a very slow week, and on the last morning, we got hammered by terrible weather, with rain, snow, sleet, and sustained winds of over sixty miles an hour. I couldn't imagine worse bowhunting weather.

But not to be deterred, we went out anyway. After all, it was the last day, and you can't kill 'em from the couch, I always say. Three of us set out that morning to brave the weather. Meanwhile Tony decided to stay back at the cabin and protect our valuables from aliens and bands of thieving Sasquatches.

We had spread out along some of the numerous elk travel routes in hopes of intercepting one. These trails would lead from the alfalfa fields in the bottom's up to their high-country day beds. By eight thirty that morning, we were all soaked and frozen. I decided to call it quits since we hadn't seen a thing all morning. The wind, snow and sleet were all blowing horizontally as I walked down to the guys locations. The nasty wind made even the idea of trying to shoot an arrow accurately absolutely absurd. Maybe, Tony wasn't so dumb after all!

As we stood in the flat-bottom coulee discussing our options, I spotted a small band of elk crest the ridge. PTL! They were coming our way. I hollered, "Get down," as I crouched down behind

Kent. Kent was kneeling down, facing me. He was grinning away, completely clueless as to what was going on. With nothing bigger than sage brush to hide behind, Kent was as good an option as any. We hid in plain sight until the herd dropped into a draw. Then it was every man for himself.

As soon as the elk disappeared from view, I took off running straight at them. Jim and Kent also scattered for cover. I was panting heavily after doing my hundred-yard dash in those heavy, wet clothes. I climbed halfway up a short, steep ridge and quickly sat down behind a sage bush.

The elk would have to follow the game trail that passed about ten yards below me. A deep, steep washout would force the elk to stay on that trail. The wind was still whipping at sixty mph according to the radio. But after my sprint, those intense winds were now blowing perfectly in my face.

I drew my bow as the lead cow rounded the corner. She surprisingly stopped broadside on the trail just below me. Should I? I wondered to myself. A cow is certainly better than an unfilled tag. Nope! Even though it was the last day, I still wanted that bull. I let her continue on, as she headed over toward my buddies. One by one, the rest of the band of elk filtered past me. The last elk to pass by was a six-by-six bull. He was a little busted up with two broken tines, but I really didn't care. He would be the fulfillment of so many years of dreams! As he came up the trail, I thought this just might work. He even stopped broadside right where I wanted him to. He was so close even the wind shouldn't affect my shot.

I was at full draw, but to my horror, I couldn't see the bull. Between the wind, rain, snow, sleet, and my panting from the hundred yard dash, my coke-bottle glasses were so fogged up that I couldn't see through them at all. I frantically tried blowing up on them. I wiggled my nose in a fruitless attempt to slide my glasses down my nose. I even tried tilting my head to look over or around my optics, but all to no avail. Finally some rain or sweat dripped down, washing just enough fog off my left lens that I could sort of get a glimpse of my sight pins. I did my best to pick a spot, and twang! My arrow was off.

And I mean way off! I am right eye dominant, and I just took a foggy shot with only my left eye. I couldn't believe I missed him cleanly at point-blank range. The bull must have caught the movement and leaped out of the gate like he was a part of a PBR event. The bull then ran off around the corner and stopped on the other side of the washout, looking back at me. He was still in bow range, but not in those high winds. After a few minutes, the perplexed little herd simply walked off up to some heavier cover, never really knowing what had just happened.

I snapped back to reality as I thought, hopeless, Why even bother? I didn't think this trip would produce, and it certainly hadn't! I didn't want to come and now I'd wasted all this time and money that I didn't have and for what? Another week of failed attempts. I was really wallowing in self-pity as I whined to the Lord. I kept asking him why I was there. Why, if I wasn't going to get one? I didn't have the time or money and really didn't want to come. Why, God? Why? It just didn't make any sense. Lord, you made it so clear that I was to come out here. But for what? Just more failed attempts! Why, God?

I was surprised when God answered me with his still, small voice. *Why did you come out here?* he asked.

I don't know. I guess because you told me to.

But why? God asked again.

Without thinking, I pointed behind me and I said, Because of him!

Wham! Lightbulb time!

Have you ever been so wrapped up in yourself or what you were doing or failing to do that you totally missed why God had you there in the first place? For the first time that day, I realized this hunt was not about me. It was really not about me at all. It was all about Pete, my friend who was going through the worst time of his life and desperately needed a listening ear, some words of encouragement, along with some fresh mountain air.

Wow! Duh! I felt awful! I smiled and apologized to God and to Pete. When we made it back to the truck, the rain sputtered to a halt. As we ate our lunches, Pete asked, "What's the game plan, boss?"

I replied, "There's one more area we haven't tried yet. Let's give it another shot. After all, I'm an eleventh-hour success kinda guy, and this is our last afternoon."

The morning rain had been replaced by light flurries. After switching to our driest available clothing, we were off again with a fresh new attitude.

After a good hike in, we came to the crest of a ridge and set up along a small lake. My first bugle was quickly answered by a herd bull's screams. We then enjoyed forty-five minutes of cat and mouse until the wind finally gave us away.

The next valley we tried produced another bull. A half hour later we were again betrayed by swirling winds. The third valley revealed yet another bull. We worked this bull until darkness set in. As we hiked out that night, I bugled one last time from atop a ridge. We smiled as there were at least six different bulls singing away. We had finally found them!

At four o'clock the next morning, I was busy making breakfast. My buddy Pete slowly emerged from the basement. He was creeping up the stairs in a very sloth-like fashion. I asked joyfully, "You ready for some guttin', braggin', and draggin'?"

He replied, "Bud, I barely made it up the stairs this morning. I just can't make that mountain again!"

I had been running on a combination of fumes and sheer determination and had pushed him to the point of exhaustion. He then made the comment, "Hunting is supposed to be fun!" His comment stopped me in my tracks. Yesterday was fun, but it had also sucked the last bit of life out of him.

Instead of trying to squeeze in one last morning, we instead decided to wash the dishes and clean the house we were staying in. I also apparently locked the owners out as we left that morning. Oops! Sorry!

Pete then asked, "So where are we headed?"

"Just rest up, bud! We have about a six-hour drive ahead of us to a friend's cabin. My mule deer tag is good there, and I'll show you some new country."

The scenery was breathtaking as we hiked around the breaks that evening. We even made sure we took several good talk breaks in the process. The next morning we hunted and hiked around again before taking off for home. The deer didn't cooperate that morning, but ironically, the elk did. I guess that's why there is always next year and we keep trying.

Overall, we had a very good trip, despite never actually seeing an elk in the Swan. We walked through some of the most beautiful country God ever created. We had close encounters with bobcats and cougars. Our arrows also put the smack down on several grouse. On our nightly hike outs, we were often serenaded by wolf packs. We came back physically exhausted but emotionally recharged. Could it really have been any better?

I can only imagine how our trip would have ended had I given up that afternoon as I wallowed in self-pity. What benefit would I have been to Pete? What would my testimony have been like?

It really is a battlefield of the mind. It's our choice to be content in all of our circumstances or whine like a spoiled child. I had momentarily lost sight of Jesus's greatest commandments: love God, love others.

Do nothing from selfishness or empty conceit, but with humility of mind regard one another as more important than yourselves; do not merely look out for your own personal interests, but also for the interests of others. (Philippians 2:3–4)

Keeping this in mind will keep your attitude one of gratitude.

CHAPTER 16

Rattled!

Ground blinds have come a long way in the last forty years. Back in the seventies my ground blinds didn't consist of much more than a log or stump to sit on. After picking my log in a location that offered a good vantage point, I would then weave branches and other foliage around my seat of luxury. The foliage did a great job of breaking up my silhouette, as well as masking many of my movements. Another benefit was that the thicker you made your cover, the more wind you could break. Ahhh, let me rephrase that. The thicker you wove your blind, the less the north wind could slice through you.

Snow and single-digit temperatures seemed to be the norm for opening weekend of deer season in northern Wisconsin. Most years, I would get dropped off by my uncle well before first light and get picked up well after dark. Those were some long, cold days for a teenage boy to sit alone in the woods.

The one exception was my first hunt ever. My dad actually accompanied me on that first deer hunt. That morning will forever be imprinted upon my mind. The fresh falling snow had the north woods resembling a Michael Sieve painting. Everyone in camp was up and gone long before first light—that is, except Dad and me.

Apparently breakfast dishes were far more important than getting in the woods early. Besides Dad said it would be much warmer after the sun came up.

Well, after the sun made its glorious appearance, we finally made our way out toward Dad's secret spot. The deep snow made each of our steps a labor of love as my excitement level soared. I had dreamed of this day for my entire short life. I could hardly believe it was finally becoming a reality. I was incredibly pumped up!

Every so often Dad would stop and carefully look around. Yup, we could still see the cabin. Not quite far enough yet. We continued to hike over the next hill and around the bend.

"Here we are!" Dad said. We had finally arrived at Dad's secret spot, which, by the way, was all of a hundred yards from the cabin.

"Really, Dad?" I asked. "The A-frame is right over there!" I pointed.

"I know," he said. "The deer will never expect anyone this close!" he responded joyfully! "Besides, just think of how convenient our lunch break will be!" he said, grinning from ear to ear.

We promptly wiped the snow off a fallen tree. This frozen maple would be my lounge chair for the remainder of the day. Dad and I began to study the terrain for the slightest of movements. After ten or fifteen minutes of this intense visual workout, Dad handed me the old .35 Remington and gave me instructions to wake him up if anything came along.

Bears have been known to hibernate out in the open, often with no cover greater than a depression in the terrain. My dad would make a good bear! As his snoring echoed through the woods, I began to question if this is really what hunting was all about. Three hours later, Dad woke up, and I had the chance to ask him that very question.

He said, "Look around. Have you ever seen anything more beautiful?"

The evergreen branches were hanging low from the weight of the freshly fallen snow. "Listen," he said. "What do you hear?"

The deafening silence was broken ònly by the occasional chickadee or red squirrel's chatter. A handful of distant shots over the course of the morning were the only real evidence that man even existed apart from us.

By now you've come to the conclusion that my dad was not a diehard hunter. He simply went along because I wanted him to. Dad loved the camaraderie of deer camp but really had no desire to fill a tag. Dad did love the beauty of God's creation as well as fellowshipping with its creator. As for me? I love these things too. I loved being out there that morning, even though we never saw a deer. I was making cherished memories with my dad.

I was reliving those memories as I sat in a state-of-the-art camo pop-up blind. It is now many years since that first hunt, and my .35 Remington had been exchanged for a compound bow. That not-so-comfy log had been replaced by a five-gallon pail complete with a snap-on padded seat. My dad had long since gone on to hang out with his maker. And my quarry? It was now Rocky Mountain elk, rather than north woods deer. The frigid single-digit temperatures were now sweltering in the upper nineties.

It was September in Montana, and it was miserably hot. I had placed my blind near a cattle tank that was surrounded by elk tracks and rubs. My expectations started to soar as I could hear a herd coming in to drink. The herd turned out to be a herd of cattle. While some drank, others sniffed at my blind. Some would snort or bellow at me. One old cow even stuck her head right in the blind's window. When she spooked, she made a hasty retreat, attempting to take the blind with her.

After they finally left, my hopes again began to lift as the area began to quiet down. I could hear something approaching from the west. This something turned out to be an old Ford pickup. It came complete with a crusty old cowboy checking the tank's water level.

I could only laugh as the cowboy started doing this weird, head-bob thing as he stared at my blind. Apparently satisfied it wasn't placed there by aliens, he continued on his mission as he bounced off across the prairie. It was almost dark, and my fun-o-meter was nowhere near pegged.

Dark blinds will absorb the sun's heat, and on a sunny mid-nineties day, they are sweltering inside. I had long since emptied both my Nalgenes, and I was seriously getting dehydrated. I had stripped down to my boxers hours ago in an attempt to stay cool. It was time to call it a day as darkness closed in.

Dressed in shorts and tennis shoes, I trekked off toward the truck in the dark as I fantasized about quenching my thirst. My blind was packed up neatly and strapped to my back. With my bow in one hand and my bucket in the other, I headed off.

I couldn't imagine the stars ever being brighter as I crossed the prairie on that two track road. My fantasies about the water in the truck were suddenly interrupted by a deafening rattle. In mid stride I hit reverse so fast I almost dropped my transmission. With my heart in my throat, I leaped backwards about ten yards! I fumbled frantically in my fanny pack for my headlamp. With the trail now fully illuminated, I proceeded back down it. There in front of me was a three-foot prairie rattler. I could see where I hit reverse, and I realized I was only inches away from stepping on him. Hmmm? Now what should I do?

Last year I had brought my sons home a horned toad. The last thing Mark asked me before I left this year was to bring him home a rattlesnake. I was holding in my left hand a five-gallon pail complete with a snap-on lid. If I brought my kids home a live rattlesnake, I would undoubtedly get the coolest dad ever award.

As I pondered the image of me on stage, receiving such a grand award, another image popped into my head—this one was of my very angry wife. My wife does not like snakes! And I was pretty certain she would not approve of such a spectacular gift for my boys. I weighed out all the arguments for the greatest dad award versus the bone-headed father/husband award. I also took into consideration all the pros and cons of capturing a live rattlesnake. Sadly, better judgment won out. His tail would have to suffice.

"Ask, and it will be given to you; seek, and you will find; knock, and it will be opened to you. For everyone who asks receives, and he who seeks finds, and to him who knocks it will be opened. Or what man is there among you who, when his son asks for a loaf, will give him a stone? Or if he asks for a fish, he will not give him a snake, will he? If you then, being evil, know how to give good gifts to your children, how much more will your Father who is in heaven give what is good to those who ask Him! (Matthew 7:7-11)

Jesus explained that good fathers give good gifts. They don't give them anything evil or harmful because they love us and only want what's best for us. My dad went hunting with me because he loved me. I gave Mark a good gift and not a harmful one because I love him. God only gives good gifts to his children. No matter what you've received in life or whatever you are going through, if it's bad or harmful, be assured that it is not from God. It's really bad theology to blame a good Holy God for things he would not do.

James 1:17 says, "Every good thing given and every perfect gift is from above coming down from the father of lights, with whom there is no variation or shifting shadows."

It doesn't matter what kind of earthly father you may have had. Your heavenly Father is perfect. He loves you unconditionally and only gives his children good gifts. Take time today and thank your heavenly Father for all the blessings in your life.

CHAPTER 17

A Piece of Stupid

Let's be honest—we've all done things that, in hindsight, were not our most shining moments. The last words spoken by any redneck are usually, "Hey, watch this" or "Here, hold my beer." Usually, it's a combination of these two. Now don't misunderstand me—I'm not picking on rednecks. I have been informed many times that I am one!

I spent many years working as a sheriff's chaplain. During that time, I worked with both the deputies as well as the inmates. I spent countless hours counseling and doing Bible studies with those inmates. During that time, I heard many unbelievable stories as well as many incredible excuses—so many, in fact, that I could be considered an expert in stupid!

No, I'm not trying to be judgmental, and we all make mistakes. As I previously stated, we are all guilty of doing a piece of stupid now and then. Early in our conversations, I usually explain to an inmate that the only thing that separates his sins from mine is that someone decided that his sins (stupid acts) were against the law and mine weren't. That puts us on a level playing field. Their defenses drop and they see me as a friend and not a foe.

One of my latest "I can't believe I did that!" moments came during a recent fall bear hunt. Wisconsin bear tags are few and far between. I've only managed to draw four tags in the last thirty-two years of applying. Tags are allotted on a preference point system. This means that each year that you apply, you are awarded one point. The unit I hunt requires eight to nine preference points before you can receive a coveted tag.

Wisconsin does have a thriving bear population, but it also has a vast number of hunters applying for those limited amount of tags. When you finally do get drawn, your life revolves around trying to fill that tag—gathering bait, placing baits and stands, checking cameras, talking to locals, as well as talking to guides. These can add up to a great amount of time and money invested.

How will you hunt? Will you be sitting over baits or running them with dogs? Sorry, guys, visibility is limited in the north woods to about twenty yards, so spot-and-stalk hunting simply is not an option. Most hunters will require locals to bait for them, or the other option is finding someone with dogs who is willing to work around your schedule. Then you have to ask the question, are they reliable?

There is a lot riding on those few hours you will finally be able to trek out with your bow or gun. Failure means another decade wait before you get another shot at filling a tag. The idea of "there's always next year" just isn't an option for most folks on a limited budget.

The pressure we feel to succeed is very real, whether it is self-imposed or from a spouse who doesn't understand why you would want to shoot Yogi or Boo-boo in the first place.

My last tag came at either the best of times or the worst of times. For the first time ever, I had the fall off to hunt. I could finally be selective and put in the time needed to harvest a big bear. The kicker was, I also drew my first Montana bull tag in five years, so instead of a five-week bear hunt, it was shaved down to a five-day bear hunt.

I had three active bait sites going into the season. I was baiting one, which was getting hit occasionally at best. Rob was baiting another, which was hit sporadically, but his pictures did include a few shooters.

Then there was George's bait. All I can say is wow! Every day for the last month, it was totally cleaned up. His trail cam pics showed about a dozen different bears hitting that bait. And they included a few dandies, one of which would rival the state record. Wisconsin, by the way, boasts some of the biggest black bears found anywhere. Several bears are harvested annually weighing six to seven hundred pounds!

The best part was, that big bear was coming in during daylight hours. The problem with big bears is that they are often sporadic as well as nocturnal. This big bear was sporadically true to form, only showing up about every week or so. But just knowing such a beast lived in the area kept my adrenaline flowing.

There were also a few three to four hundred–pounders that were definitely arrow worthy. Needless to say, I was pumped! I had eaten my last two bear tags, but this year was promising to be great!

Opening day was perfect, sixty-five degrees and sunny, with a slight north wind. I made the mile-and-a-half trek through the swamp with a bounce in my step. The trail camera pictures showed virtually all the bear activity was either in the late afternoon or after dark.

I baited and settled into my stand at three o'clock in the afternoon. About four o'clock, a small bear splashed across the creek behind me. He then circled downwind before disappearing back into the tag alders along the creek. The woods I was hunting were a mixture of tag alders, maples, berry brush, and poplar slashing. My visibility was limited to roughly twenty-five yards at best. It was a real joy to watch this little guy pass under my stand at only eight yards.

An hour later, a bigger bear came in from the north. Cautiously, he approach the bait. After deciding all was well, he stood on his hind legs and began rocking the logs back and forth until they tipped over, exposing his supper. I laughed as he ran full-tilt away as the logs came crashing over.

He came back in and fed for about fifteen minutes before spooking back off to the north. A larger shooter bear was approaching from the south. My heart was really pounding while he hung up in the brush about twenty yards away. After a few minutes of scent checking, the big bear left the way he had come in. All the scent control systems in the world will only fool a bear's nose for so long. That first evening ended with five bear sightings, three of which actually came into the bait. All three were smaller bears of two hundred pounds or less.

We had been inundated by rain over the last few weeks, and although my hunts were rain free, the swamp itself was overflowing. The four-wheeler trail I walked in on was incredibly muddy. In spots it had over a foot of running water covering it. As I plodded along on my second afternoon, my rubber knee boots got stuck in the mud. As I struggled to free myself, I lost my balance and fell forward. I somehow managed to not face-plant or drop my bow. Praise the Lord! But I lost both of my boots to the muck. Although I did recover them, I ultimately surrendered my socks to the mud.

The next mile or so of my hike I was barefoot, as I carried my boots. I was hoping my feet would somehow dry out before I reached my stand. My wife continually questions my sanity as she says, "And you call that fun?" Heck yeah it's fun! After all, that's the way the Indians did it. It's called traditional archery.

The second night ended with only one small bear sighting and two sore feet. I was getting nervous. I had heard five shots the first afternoon and two shots on the second. That didn't include any bears harvested by bowhunters. I was starting to wonder just how many shooter bears could possibly be within earshot of my tree stand. Later that evening as I filled up my truck, one of those shots I had heard pulled in for gas and ice. The beautiful bear tipped the scales at just over four hundred pounds.

The third night I saw two bears and heard two more shots. One of those shots was just over on the other side of the creek, less than a forty away. It was time for a change. I decided Saturday I would sit all day at Rob's. A new location along with uneducated bears just might be the answer.

Rob's turned out to be a bust. I never saw a bear and had only the constant buzzing of mosquitoes to keep me company. One big porcupine was my only warm-blooded companion that evening.

Sunday morning I received a text from George. When he had baited that morning, the camera revealed two shooters had come in Saturday afternoon while I was at Rob's. I think we've all experienced the frustrations of the wrong place at the right time. Well, Sunday night was my last night to hunt. Tomorrow morning we are heading to Montana with or without a bear.

So back to George's I would go. They apparently didn't harvest all the bears, and the last minute or eleventh-hour success has been my mantra for many years. Tonight would be the night!

As I snuck into the bait that afternoon, I was glad to see nothing had hit the bait since George had placed it that morning. The afternoon was warm, in the seventies, and I had worked up a good sweat as I walked in. To make matters worse, the wind was out of the east, so my usual stand wouldn't work. The bait was directly downwind of it. Thankfully, George had originally set up a double ladder stand just south of the bait that would work. It was short, only about ten feet high, and had a shooting rail around it. Some tattered camo hung from it, offering me some cover. It was not an ideal setup but would have to do.

The night started slow with only one bear, "Ralph," showing up. Ralph was a small 150-pound bear. He showed up every night I sat in that stand. I really enjoyed watching his antics, and I had no desire to shoot him. No, not even on the last night. I called him Ralph because he would often rest both arms over the hollow stump while sticking his whole head in the stump. It really looked like he was praying to the porcelain god, hence the name Ralph. Ralph finally wandered off about six thirty. The eleventh hour had finally arrived.

I had spent a total of twenty-eight hours in a bear stand and had seen nine bears. It was truly an awesome hunt. I dreamed of harvesting a monster with my bow, but it wasn't looking too promising. I heard a few more distant shots, and I thanked the Lord for other hunters' successes.

The memory of other bear season successes and failures flooded my mind. My last bear season was cut short after only two days. One of my parishioners in the final stages of cancer had taken a turn for the worse, and ministry comes first. I was never able to make it back up north to try again, but I had no regrets. I then reminisced about the last four days. It had really been a great hunt, and although I was a little disappointed, I didn't regret passing on all the smaller bears.

As my mind wandered, I was shaken back to reality as a black shadow moved through the woods directly to the north. Please come in! I prayed. The dry sow was incredibly cautious as she slowly circled the bait and my stand. There were less than twenty minutes left until dark, and she was coming in way too slowly. It seemed to take forever for her to finally reach the bait. When she finally did come in, she was facing me.

Come on, turn, turn, I prayed. When I had first spotted her, I stood up as she walked behind some brush. The shooting rail around the stand was in the way, so I would need to lean out while holding the bow outside of the rail to pull off a shot.

Eventually she turned, giving me a desirable quartering away, nine-yard shot. As my bow came to full draw, the cams made a slight thumping sound as they bottomed out. That sound, slight as it was, snapped her to attention, with her piercing beatty eyes she busted me. As she spun away, I took the shot. She dropped and spun in circles as I quickly nocked another arrow. I feared I had spined her, but she ran off before I could even draw back again. Being unsure of the shot, I quickly slid, fireman pole style, down the ladder stand with a nocked arrow. I then chased after her into the swamp. I quickly caught up to her and dispatched her with an unnecessary follow-up shot. Thank you, Jesus!

That's when reality set in. I was a hunter safety instructor, and I had just broken a lot of rules—rules I believe in and had faithfully taught. There were too many to even mention. With no desire to spend the night tracking a wounded bear through the north woods swamps, I compromised and did a lot of stupid things in the heat of the moment—stupid things that could've cost me broken bones, lacerations, or even worse, my life.

I can only thank the Lord for his protection. Ironically, as stupid as my actions were, none of my mistakes were actually against the law. But they were stupid nonetheless. We've all pulled a piece of stupid at one time or another. You may have not slid down a ladder with a nocked arrow in your hand. Maybe you've never chased a wounded bear through the woods at night with only a bow and one arrow, but I'm sure you have said or done things that you regret.

I am so happy that God forgives our sins as well as our stupidity. I'm so thankful he doesn't hold our sins against us. If we are in Christ Jesus, we are forgiven.

If we say that we have no sin, we are deceiving ourselves and the truth is not in us. If we confess our sins, He is faithful and righteous to forgive us our sins and to cleanse us from all unrighteousness. (1 John 1:8–9)

Therefore there is now no condemnation for those who are in Christ Jesus. (Romans 8:1)

That means no matter what kind of stupid you've pulled, Jesus is faithful to forgive all those who ask. Go ahead and ask him to forgive you today!

CHAPTER 18

Right Brain, Left Brain

For bear hunters, one of the worst things that can happen is for a sow with cubs to discover your bait. Let me explain it this way. My wife and I were blessed with three hungry boys. I remember well the look of fear and terror that would come across the faces of buffet hosts as the boys rushed through the door. Any hope of profit quickly vanished as the boys filled their plates up for the fourth time.

My dad also had three sons, and likewise, we were all skinny as a rail. My dad would often describe us as looking like hockey sticks with hair. Dad came to the conclusion, and much to the chagrin of my mother, he would tell people that we never gained any weight because our butts were bigger than our mouths and everything would just fall through. Sorry, Mom! Buffets actually held such a dear place in our hearts that one of my sons actually cried when they closed the local Shakey's all-you-can-eat pizza buffet. Don't judge, as he was only six at the time.

What does any of this have to do with bear hunting? Glad you asked! Much like my boys, a bear's life revolves around it stomach. A bear will gorge itself from the time it emerges from its den each spring until it returns there in the late fall or winter.

Just a side note, not all black bears hibernate. Hibernation is more dependent upon food availability than temperatures or snow depth. Much like our Thanksgiving dinner, after the food is gone, it's time to go sleep it off. Northern bears may sleep up to six or seven months a year, while bears in the Florida Everglades may not hibernate at all.

Northern bears need to feed. They will gorge themselves as much as possible during the six months they are awake. This makes baiting a very productive method of hunting. The majority of baited bears will be nocturnal, while still other bait sites will be taken over by sows and cubs, so baiting is certainly no guarantee of success. By the way, both cubs and their mothers are protected by law, so relax, bunny huggers. I wouldn't dream of shooting either of them!

A single bear can travel great distances each day as it searches for food. At the same time, a cub can't travel too far from the buffet line on its short little legs. So when mom finds a good buffet for her hungry boys, she will camp out on it. A big bear is certainly not afraid of a sow with cubs, but big mama will be the first one in the buffet line, and her family will stay there until the restaurant is closed. Any bear that shows up afterward will find the buffet line empty and will soon stop coming in. So when a sow and cubs takes over your bait, your best option is to relocate at least a mile away.

A few years back, I had two active baits going. Both were getting cleaned up regularly, but only nighttime visits were occurring. Several weeks into the season, the bears remained nocturnal. I tried everything I could think of, from increasing and reducing the amount of bait I placed, to the time and type of bait I was using, all in an attempt to entice them out of the shadows before dark. It was all to no avail.

A local realtor heard of my predicament and offered up the use of his deer stand. He complained the bears were cleaning up his corn pile daily. I was more than happy to help this poor fellow out of his predicament. After he showed me around his extensive property, I made plans to come back after work the following day.

The next day was a perfect autumn day. The fall colors could not have been more breathtaking against the deep blue skies. The temperature was hovering around sixty degrees. Many of the rolling hills had been clear-cut within the last year or two, making the new growth only a few feet tall. There were also patches of thick red berry brush mixed in among the young poplars.

As I hiked along the logging trail, I spotted three black forms down by the bait. The bait was located at the bottom of the hill where the clear-cut met up with a large hemlock swamp. They were still about 150 yards away as I made my plan.

The wind was perfect, blowing directly into my face. I sat down and took off my boots, dropped my backpack, and nocked an arrow. I would need to sneak to within thirty yards of the bears. I practiced daily with my long bow and found thirty yards to be my maximum effective range. As I crept up on them, I felt like one of the hunters of old, stalking in on my prey in my stocking feet with a stick bow. It only took about fifteen minutes to close the distance. I had approached to within about twenty-five yards, and they still had no clue I was there.

To prevent the shooting of cubs or sows with cubs, Wisconsin has a minimum standard length of forty-two inches. This is measured from the bears nose to its tail. You are not allowed to shoot any bear measuring less than forty-two inches or shoot any bear accompanying a bear of less than forty-two inches. The two smaller bears were right at the forty-two inch mark. I was really unsure if they were big cubs or legal yearlings. She was big for a sow, in the three hundred–pound range. I wanted her, but I didn't want to risk shooting her if the smaller bears were in fact cubs. Since it's virtually impossible to get a live bear to stand still while you stretch your tape measure down their back, I let caution win out.

I stood up and hollered at the bears, "Get out of here! Go on, beat it!"

The smaller ones immediately ran up my tree—yes, the very one my stand was in. Mama just turned and looked at me. Then instead of running away as I thought she would, she stood up to get a better look. This certainly wasn't working out as I had planned. The more I walked toward her and yelled, the more anxious she became!

After I walked to within twenty yards, I decided I was close enough. She apparently did too as she dropped to all fours and ran over by her young'uns. She was huffing and puffing, woofing out orders as she went. The smaller bears remained frozen, death gripping my tree. And like any good mother would, the sow soon tired of their disobedience and swatted one of the youngsters on the rear end, knocking him out of the tree. He proceeded to race off into the swamp. The other bear apparently learned from his brother's whopping and quickly came down willingly. The trio then crashed off into the swamp, never to be seen again.

I've often marveled at the mysterious nature of the female gender. They often don't respond as I would have expected. Frequently they respond in the very opposite way than what I had hoped for or expected they would. Let me explain.

This fall I was watching a doe work her way through the buck brush hillside above me. I sat motionless as I watched her gracefully slip through the thorny trees. She eventually stopped in one of my shooting lanes. After glancing my way, she froze. Something seemed out of place to her. That large camouflage blob in the tree just didn't look quite right. What could it be? Sniff, sniff. No odor. Her supersensitive ears didn't hear anything. It was not moving, but something was just not right.

She reasoned, *I shall stare at it for twenty minutes while I stomp my feet in annoyed disapproval! I shall then snort, alerting every deer within earshot of my displeasure. If that doesn't work, I shall turn away and stomp off in disgust!*

Does this sound familiar? This is the most common response from doe encounters across the nation. If a doe detects something is amiss, she wants to know exactly what it is that troubles her. She will not ignore it, nor will she leave, at least until she figures out what it is.

Later that same morning, I cracked my antlers together in hopes a buck had wandered into earshot. Within minutes, I caught sight of a buck sneaking along the same trail the doe had taken. He eventually stopped in the same shooting lane the doe had.

He glanced my way before continuing on his way. The beautiful young eleven-pointer would receive a free pass today. He was a perfectly symmetrical five-by-five with an extra four-inch brow tine. At only two and a half years old, I was sure he would mature into a Boone and Crockett candidate if given the chance too.

As the buck walked away, I grunted.` The buck turned and circled downwind of me. When he eventually arrived downwind, it only took one good whiff for him to decide enough was enough, and he briskly walked away. This is a common response a buck will exhibit when something is just not quite right. A buck, bull, or boar will either sneak or run off. Seldom are their tails up, and seldom do they snort or stomp. Why? I believe self-preservation is the answer.

Facts are facts to a male. They usually don't care why something is amiss, just that it is, so they beat feet out of there, no questions asked. Females, on the other hand, want to know all the whys. They often want to confirm their suspicions with their other senses while they let the whole world know of their displeasure.

Truth be told, I believe a lot of does get shot because their curiosity has spooked the other deer while annoying the hunter.

God created them male and female. (Genesis 1:27)

God created us differently, whether human or animals. Males and females are programmed differently, we're motivated differently, and we think differently and usually respond differently. That's okay! It's not wrong; it's just different. If God wanted us all the same, he would've created us all the same.

I recently tried to plan ahead and fulfill my wife's need to know. Our friends had just been blessed with a new granddaughter. As my friend shared his joy with me, I asked him the questions I knew my wife would be asking me. How long was she? What did she weigh? How long was her labor?

His response to each question was, "I don't know! But she had ten fingers and ten toes!" As long as all the necessary parts were there, the details didn't matter.

Generally speaking, females, whatever the species, tend to be more about relationships and family, and they signal to the world when something doesn't seem quite right. It's a protective nature God programmed into the female's DNA.

Males have a much higher mortality rate than females, regardless of the species. As a result, males tend to be more motivated by self-preservation. The need to rest, feed, and breed dominate their existence. This behavior doesn't seem to bother does, but in humans it's just wrong. We weren't created to be a love 'em and leave 'em species.

As humans we need to understand the opposite sex's programming so we can better balance our relationships with them. We are not animals, so we shouldn't act like them. Understanding the opposite sex's motivations and needs can help us all live in peace with each other.

As my dad often said, "Happy wife, happy life!"

CHAPTER 19

Just Say No!

Just say no! Really? Come on, do you remember the old ads trying to influence kids to stay away from drugs? Everyone from the First Lady to actors and actresses were in your face with that catchphrase. Although I appreciate their efforts, I'm not really sure how much good any of it did. After all, do our words really have any power?

Most of us have experienced lulls in our hunting action. Our hunts seldom play out like an action-packed half-hour TV show or hunting video. Hour after hour of dead time is a lot closer to reality. Oftentimes these mundane hours can lead to mundane days.

Last fall I experienced one of those hunts where you catch yourself wondering if there is any wildlife within twenty miles of you. My son and I were hunting the same area we had the previous fall.

On the previous hunt, elk were plentiful and hunters were few. Our first evening was picture perfect. We had hiked to the top of a jack pine ridge. This ridge had a truly magnificent view. Rugged mountain ranges spread out in every direction. Below us lay a thick valley, dripping with fresh elk sign. Large rubs and wallows were scattered out before us like they were dispersed from a saltshaker.

Our enthusiasm could not have been higher as we chose our perfect spots.

I was to be the caller and Mark the hunter. The choice of who was the shooter was a no-brainer. Mark had a tag and I didn't. I was armed with only my bugle tube and a video camera.

I set up Miss September on the crest of the ridge, where she could be seen for hundreds of yards from several directions. Miss September is a decoy that I carry. She folds down nicely and fits into my backpack. I usually spray her down with cow in heat urine. I then place her where she can be seen from longer distances. Having a visual aid can often entice a reluctant bull, buck, or tom into archery range.

Mark was set up south of me on the crest of the ridge. Miss September was about thirty yards behind him. I was hiding about thirty yards behind the decoy in some jack pines. The light breeze was blowing from Mark up to me.

My first bugle received an immediate response from deep down in the valley. Our hearts raced as we were reassured that bulls were still in the area. I continued to cow call, while throwing in an occasional bugle. I was really hoping to draw in one of the three distant but vocal bulls.

My eyes were drawn to a distant mountain. I watched a huge bull direct his harem across a meadow about two miles away. He had twelve cows and wanted nothing to do with the smaller six-by-six that was harassing them. I shot up a quick, "Praise the Lord" for good optics!

Awesome, I thought, *this just might be a gimme hunt.* Bulls were bugling below us. Bulls were chasing cows above us. This is what dreams are made of! I snapped back into reality as I saw Mark's head appear from behind a jack pine. After we made eye contact, he held his hand to his ear and pointed up the hill.

After many years of factory work, using chainsaws, driving motorcycles, and enjoying shooting sports, my hearing leaves a lot to be desired. Many times my hunting partners are flabbergasted that

I never heard the bugles or gobbles that were coming from "right over there" as they point violently.

This was not one of those times. This bull was coming in silently as he snuck in from behind Mark. Mark could hear the bull's hooves on the rocky ground as the bull worked his way in for a closer look. Although I couldn't see or hear the bull, I could see Mark. He was now down on one knee and at full draw. Seconds turned into minutes before Mark's aching arms forced him to let down on his bow.

At forty yards, the bull had walked through a shooting lane and stopped behind a lone jack pine. I cow called, and the bull started walking again. Mark drew back again, only to have the bull stop behind another jack pine! After holding back for what seemed like an eternity, he had to let down again. I bugled, and for the first time, the bull responded. This was the first time I was sure Mark was actually drawing on a bull and not a buck. As the bull made his way toward me, Mark skirted along below him. The bull entered another shooting lane at thirty yards. Mark again drew back on the bull, but the bull continued into some more jacks.

This time the bull stopped only thirty yards from me. I had no bow or license, which is probably why the bull offered me a great shot. The bull was a beautiful five-by-five. He would alternate from looking at Mark to looking at me. I tried to keep his attention with cow calls as Mark attempted to sneak in closer. Eventually it got too dark to shoot, and the bull simply wandered off.

That season ended with more close encounters but no filled tags. Fast forward one year—the same hunters, same area, only this time no elk. Apparently the area had been pounded by other hunters during the first two weeks of bow season. By the time the rut was on, the elk were nowhere to be found. The few elk that still remained in the area were call shy and nocturnal. After five days of hard hunting, covering about twelve miles a day, I had only seen two cows and they were a half a mile away.

Day six found us exploring some more new country. It had been drizzling all morning, dampening our clothes as well as our spirits. We would walk and call every quarter mile or so.

About ten in the morning, we stopped to suck down some trail mix when a high-pitched squeal came from above us. We quickly set up, and Mark let out some cow calls. I joined in with some of my own. We each carry about three different cow calls in an attempt to sound like a small herd rather than a single animal or some flat lander with a hoochie mama! This usually works, but the little five-by-five bull circled downwind of us before he ever came within range.

While we were in the area, I decided to show Mark a wallow I had discovered the previous year. As we approached the wallow, our hearts sank as another hunter was already there. After a short visit, we headed back toward camp, where my wife had a nice meal waiting for us. It was about eleven thirty in the morning as we trudged down the closed two track. Frustrated and dejected, we discussed our hunting options for the rest of the day and week.

As we walked along, a loud crashing sound brought us back into the moment. Expecting to see elk, I looked up just in time to see a grizzly bear charging us from above. His ears were laid back, and his brow was wrinkled as he came off that ridge at Mach1. He hit the road just eight steps from us!

Mark immediately turned and yelled, "No! Bear! Get out of here!"

The bear turned on a dime and headed up the road away from us. Mark was nocking an arrow as he ran up the road after the bear, hollering back at me, "Was that a grizzly?"

I said, "I think so!" as I chased after him.

We both knew it was, but Mark had a black bear tag and just wanted to make sure. Really? Chasing a bear with a bow? Yes, really! See chapter 17, the one I entitled "A Piece of Stupid." Like father like son, I guess.

I have no idea why that bear charged us, but I am certain of a few things. One, if he wanted us, he could've had us. There is no way I would've had time to pull either my pistol or my bear spray—and I do carry both! Second, Mark's yelling is what turned the bear. Is there really power in our words? Well, something made him turn on a dime, and that's all we really did.

Third, it's always good to be bear aware! Supposedly grizzlies are not common to that particular area of the state. Ironically, we ran into the wallow hunter a few days later, and he had a similar incident five years earlier on that same ridge. He had to shoot several times in front of the bear before it finally turned.

As I snapped pictures of the location of my encounter, my mind raced back to another experience I had with my father-in-law many years earlier. We were hiking around his new property in West Virginia. As we rounded a corner, we were greeted by two vicious pit bulls. They ran at us, snarling and growling. These dogs had a bad reputation as they had bitten several of the neighbors. They had also attacked and killed some of the local pets. Now they were coming straight at us!

A loud, authoritative, "No!" came from my father-in-law. "No!" he repeated as the charging dogs screeched to a halt.

They continued to growl and snap their teeth, but they stopped running at us. Every time they would start at us, again we would holler, "No!" As we continued past them, they continued to growl and snap their teeth, but they were stopped short in their attack. They submitted to our authority and the word no.

It's amazing how our words do have power! There are many powerful quotes in the Bible like the following:

- "Life and death are in the power of the tongue." (Proverbs 18:21).
- "Greater is he who is in you than he who is in the world." (1 John 4:4).
- "I can do all things through Christ who strengthens me." (Phil. 4:13).
- "Jesus said, In my name they will cast out demons." (Mark 16:17).
- "Even the demons are subject to his name." (Luke 10:17).
- "Submit to God, resist the devil and he will flee from you!" (James 4:7).

Those dogs unwillingly submitted to a human authority who boldly said no. Even a dumb dog knows what no means and will reluctantly submit to it.

The devil has every right to attack us but must willingly submit to the authority of Jesus's name. As humans we are under the devil's thumb, but as Christians, he is under our heel. Submit to God, resist the devil, and he will flee from you. Like an old piece of gum, keep him stuck to the tread of your boots. To keep him there, it's up to you to tell him no in Jesus's name.

Maybe "Just say no!" does work.

CHAPTER 20

Mentors

October 10, 2015, was a beautiful fall evening. I was sitting in one of my favorite deer stands, and beside me sat a very excited young man. It was Jim's first deer hunt. Today was also the first day of Wisconsin's annual youth hunt. Jim's older brother John was sitting just up the field from us. Our stands were located along a standing cornfield. My trail cam photos had revealed the presence of numerous bucks that would make any twelve-year-old proud. The camera also revealed the presence of a few dandies that would make even this old preacher proud.

The secluded field was surrounded by woods and boasted many deer and turkeys. The double-stands location made for easy access from the road. I would often hunt it when my time was limited because I could access it without spooking any deer that may have already entered the field. The only thing this stand requires is a south wind.

This stand was also the only double wide I owned, making it the perfect choice for coaching a young hunter through a shot process or a romantic evening out with my wife.

Seriously, think about it—gorgeous fall colors, sitting side-by-side with your sweetheart watching a beautiful sunset. It's an awesome cheap date, providing, of course, that you can keep them quiet.

If you choose to try a night out with a special someone, here are some tips that will help make it an enjoyable time. First, make sure you pick the right circumstances. Evenings are a much better choice than forcing a non-morning person out of bed at four in the morning!

The stand should be a relatively short walk from your vehicle. The stand should be either a safe and stable double stand or a spacious ground blind. Next, it has to be late enough in the year that the frost has killed off most of the mosquitoes and ticks and yet early enough, that fall temperatures are still modest, say in the sixties or whatever you may consider comfortable. Let them bring a silenced cell phone to game on. It will help them to pass the time, and it's not worth the fight. The number one goal is that your companion enjoy the experience or their first one will likely be their last one.

What will you get out of it? Great memories, the possibility of future dates, and maybe, just maybe, a new hunting partner.

As Jim and I settled in for our evening hunt, my mind drifted back to many past hunts that centered around this stand. There was Dave's first bow buck. After many close calls, Dave's arrow had finally found home. Even at fifty years old, he was every bit as excited as any twelve-year-old boy!

Then there was Rocky. Rocky's love for bowhunting was interrupted by work schedules and shoulder injuries. But after a ten-year hiatus, my brother joined me for a fall hunt. His smile was clearly evident from across the field as he paced back and forth looking for his arrow. His smile grew even bigger when we found his eight-point buck fifteen minutes later.

Then there was the ten-pointer I rattled in for Mark. The whole stand was shaking as the buck circled the decoy. No video game will ever match the excitement that a thirteen-year-old boy will feel as a big buck sniffs your decoy at fifteen yards. Mark stood on wobbly knees as he drew back, waiting for me to whisper now.

Crunch, crunch, crunch! The distinct sound of a deer walking snapped me back to reality. I slowly glanced behind me to the right, then back to the left. My eyes straining to see our noisy quarry. The deer was downwind and only yards behind us. As I started to whisper instructions to Jim.

"Buck! buck! buck!" Jim hollered as he swung my old .35 Remington around. The nice eight-pointer was gone in a flash! When I finished laughing, I suggested to Jim that he might want to try moving a little slower and quieter next time.

When it comes to mentoring, our attitudes and responses to situations is usually the only thing separating a good experience from a bad one. After all, hunting is supposed to be fun. When we take it too seriously, we can be a real killjoy. This will undoubtedly turn a young hunter off. I usually tell a young hunter that misses happen to us all. It's okay, and I won't be mad at you. My laughing and reassuring shoulder squeeze reinforced to Jim that I meant what I said and hunting is supposed to be fun. That experience was fun, whether or not a shot was ever fired. An animal doesn't have to take a dirt nap for a hunt to be successful.

John's first hunt went a little different than Jim's had. A few years earlier, it was John who was sitting next to me in that double stand. As the sun began to set that evening, I wondered if any deer would show up. The thick alfalfa field was normally filled with deer. Tonight was different though, as the farm had just hosted our church's annual hayride. Just an hour before, wagon loads of noisy kids circled these woods and fields. Although I thought our chances were slim, they were still a lot better than not trying at all.

As I sat pondering the day's activities, John nudged me. A pair of does slowly walked out across the field. "Too far," I whispered. They would have to feed a lot closer than that to be in good iron sight range. Our prayers were answered as the deer slowly fed our way, eighty, seventy, sixty yards and closing!

John had rested my old rifle across the shooting rail when the deer were first spotted. His cheek now pressed down tightly against the stock.

"Now?" he whispered.

"No, just wait."

"Now?"

"Just wait!" The does were now at fifty yards, but we were quickly losing daylight! That's when I gave him the go-ahead. The lead doe turned broadside as I whispered instructions.

"Pick a spot behind the front shoulder and slowly squeeze the trigger whenever you are ready."

Silence followed, seemingly endless silence, or at least on my end. Meanwhile John was quietly saying, "Now? Now! Now!"

Each time his plea was getting a little bit louder, but still too quiet for me to hear. "Now? Now! Now!"

"Okay, shoot!"

Bang! At the shot the doe jumped and kicked her hind legs in the air as she raced into the woods. Then silence. The only noise to be heard was the ringing in my ears.

"You got her! Good shot!"

His huge grin was well worth a little more hearing loss on my end. We searched earnestly for blood, but none could be found. Eventually we had to give up the search. Our emotions went from mountaintop highs to death valley lows. I was positive he had made a perfect heart shot, but I simply could not find any sign of a hit. She'd been standing in the hay field only ten steps from where she entered a massive tangle of blackberry and buck brush. Trailing her through that jungle left both of us frustrated, bleeding, and wearing a crown of thorns.

When I dropped John off at his home, I reassured him I would do my best to find her in the morning. I'm still not sure how much he actually slept that night. The next morning as John headed off to school, I headed off to the woods. I searched prayerfully as I wrestled my way through the brush without finding a drop of blood that wasn't mine. As my search circles widened, my optimism shrunk.

I was elated when I finally spotted the telltale sign of a white belly. John had his first deer! She had traveled less than seventy-five yards after taking his perfect heart shot. I quickly called his mother, who was a teacher at John's middle school. She had him waiting at the main entrance when I arrived.

The smiling picture of him with his trophy is still one of my favorites. We spent the rest of the day processing his venison as we relived the hunt. I praise the Lord that John's mom, a public school teacher, knows the value of not letting school get in the way of a child's education.

A lot of lessons just can't be learned in the classroom. Some life skills require hands-on experience. Learning life's lessons never really ends if we have a teachable spirit. Some of these life lessons can also be very painful.

Case in point, the following spring John and I had set up for turkeys at the back of his property. Our decoys were spread out in front of us as we waited for first light. John was twelve or thirteen at the time and excited to shoot his first bird. We sat shoulder to shoulder with our backs against a large oak.

Distant gobbles broke the silence as the sky began to lighten. The cut cornfield crested sixty to seventy yards out in front of us. Turkeys could literally come from any direction without giving us much notice. The birds weren't my concern though. His gun was! I normally borrowed one of my son's twelve gauges for spring turkey. But today, the only gun available was Zak's single-shot ten gauge loaded with three-and-a-half-inch mags. Experience told me it kicked like a mule. But I reasoned to myself, when he rolls a bird, he won't even notice the kick! Ahhh, yeah? Yeah! We'll go with that?

After about an hour and a half, the gobbling had ceased and we had yet to even see a bird. I continued my hen purrs, clucks, and yelps in hopes a wary tom would eventually make an appearance. John was busy alternating between squirming and sleeping. That's when some redheads popped up over the crest of the hill. Six turkeys started to make their way toward our setup. There were four hens and two jakes. Any bearded turkey is fair game, and a jake is a great trophy for a youngster.

The ten gauge was heavy! Although it rested on John's knee, it still wobbled back and forth. One of the hens didn't like all this movement and decided it was time to head out, taking the rest of the flock with her. It was now or never! "Shoot!" Boom!

John immediately dropped the gun as he grabbed his shoulder. I quickly reloaded and handed the gun back to him. "Shoot again!" I hollered.

"No!" was his disgusted response. As the turkeys disappeared from view, I was laughing again!

He chuckled too as he continued rubbing his sore shoulder. For the record, later that summer he was gifted with a youth model twenty gauge that fit him perfectly. John has since harvested several toms and about a half a dozen deer. He's matured into an excellent young hunter. This past year he has started taking his younger brother and sister out as he now mentors them.

Opening day of the youth turkey season found John, Jilly, and me sitting in a ground blind over a cut cornfield. It was Jilly's first hunt ever, and she was packing John's twenty gauge. Boredom soon ensued, and she desired to break the monotony by shooting something. Ironic, because she is the ultimate pet/animal lover.

I jokingly encouraged her by suggesting that maybe we'd get lucky and one of Bill's cats would wander by. Boy, if looks could kill! As John and I chuckled, trying hard not to laugh audibly, Jilly just sat there scowling at us.

Her scowling was quickly changed to a smile as a big tom crested the ridge! My yelps and purrs eventually drew him into our decoys at seventeen yards. The tom had somehow managed to strut in between the pop-up blind's windows, preventing Jilly from seeing it. She had to switch positions with me and reset up in a different window, moving her chair and shooting sticks in the process.

As she nervously took aim, bang! The little gun went off. And just like her big brother, she dropped the gun, her hands now clinging tightly to her ears. I grabbed the gun and jacked another shell into the chamber before giving it back to her.

I said, "Shoot again," but she hollered, "No!" as her hands clung to her ears. John and I laughed as we recalled his hunt with the ten gauge several years earlier.

The next morning we awoke to six inches of fresh snow. Their long drive into church was not a good option, so Mom and Jilly let John sleep in until ten that morning. Then she awakened him to take her turkey hunting. Their setup would be only a hundred yards behind their home. On the walk-in, they managed to bust a big tom.

Really? John thought, as he set up the decoys. No way would they get a chance now! But five minutes later, a huge tom strutted into their set-up. Complete with her new earmuffs, our little huntress took careful aim and bang! The tom rolled, only to get up and fly off toward the house.

Excitedly the kids gathered their gear and headed back to the house. That's when they were rebuked for slamming the door. They explained they didn't slam the door? They then noticed feathers blowing across the snow-covered yard. After a quick look around, they found the big tom lying dead on the side of the house. He had slammed into and subsequently destroyed the rain gutter on his kamikaze descent.

The huge-bodied tom sported an eleven-inch beard! That eleven-year-old girl will never forget that hunt, and neither will her big brother! Later when I moved from the area, John gave me a picture/plaque he had made. It was a laser engraving of us and our two largest bow kills. Also engraved was Ecclesiastes 3, which states, "There is a time for every purpose under heaven." It was time for us to relocate, and I cried at the thought of all I was leaving behind.

When we invest our time and talents in others, we are truly the ones who ultimately get blessed. Whether I was teaching my sixty-year-old brother how to use a decoy or my fifty-year-old friend how to bowhunt or my thirteen-year-old son how to rattle or a single parent's children how to enjoy the outdoors, the joys shared, the memories, and the experiences are all benefits I received from my time invested in others.

There is a reason it's been said, "You cannot out give God." Jesus summed it up by saying, "Love God, love others!"

Who can you invest in today? You won't regret it!

CHAPTER 21

Laughter

I love to laugh! I love to joke around and make others laugh too. I come by it honestly. My dad was a huge prankster. Every night around the supper table my dad would make us all laugh with his latest jokes and pranks. He would also sprinkle in stories of the mindless acts that so-and-so did.

Dad was a wonderful, godly man, and his pranks were never dirty, mean, or hurtful. They were just funny and maybe a little mischievous. One such prank involved his in-laws, who lived in a mobile home in the backyard of our country home. They would spend their summer months in northern Wisconsin and the winter months in a trailer park in Texas. It really was not as redneck as it sounds.

Grandma and Grandpa would head north with the birds each April, and each April Dad would take handfuls of field corn and toss them up on their tin roof. Every morning about four thirty the blue jays and crows would awaken Grandma with a deafening rat-a-tat-tat. Grandpa would sleep soundly through it all. Grandpa, aside from being half deaf, was in fact in on it all.

These men reasoned that it gave Grandma something to do as she researched, just what does attract birds to a mobile home roof? When my folks retired to a lake-side cabin, people were a lot more scarce, so the victims of Dad's pranks naturally had to change. After all, my dear, sweet mother could only take so much humorous abuse.

His new targets? The local rodent population. To be precise, the local squirrels and chipmunks. His bored, engineering mind was soon put to good use. If NASA could put a man on the moon, dad could put a squirrel into orbit!

His first experiment quickly became a classic. His heavy, long exercise springs were now used to power a six-foot catapult. A small food dish screwed to the end of the launch board was all that was needed to draw in the unsuspecting victims. Dad would sit for hours holding the string that would trigger the paddle, unleashing the launch sequence.

Picture an old bald guy with an infectious smile hiding behind a tree as he waits patiently for a varmint to come in for a snack. Then on cue, thwap! Off the squirrel went! It would fly through the air with the greatest of ease like the daring young man on the flying trapeze.

Dad's goal was never to hurt the rodents. Instead, his aim was for his test dummies to clear the garage, all the trees, and overhead branches, landing the squirrel safely in the lake. I must admit, many of these test pilots didn't fare as well as Chuck Yeager did. It never ceased to amaze me the numbers of people who would join Dad by the picture window, waiting patiently for a squirrel to stop by for an afternoon in-flight meal.

Since the nut seldom falls far from the tree, my siblings and I all inherited that same quirky sense of humor. I spent about six years working maintenance at a northern Wisconsin Christian camp. No matter what your job title may be, everyone helps out in most areas around camp. When I wasn't building or fixing something, I could be found washing dishes, cleaning cabins, or instructing up at the archery range. My favorite areas to help out in, though, were teaching outdoor ed classes and speaking on wilderness trips.

One of the best parts of teaching "city folk" about creation is dispelling their Disney world mentality with the truth. I soon became aware of urban dwellers' prevalent and irrational fear of bears. Facts are facts. In the last twenty years (last time I checked anyway), only twenty-five people have been killed by black bears in all of North America. Compare that with some estimates of over six thousand deaths globally by lightning strikes each year. So if you're worried about bears, you should really consider staying off the golf course.

One day Scott, who headed up our outdoor ed ministry, asked me if I knew of any bear dens around camp. He was considering using the dens as part of a learning experience for a winter family camp. The dens I knew of were all too far away for campers to travel to, especially in knee-deep snow. But I could make one!

I assured him, "It will be great! Trust me!"

Although my dad was home with Jesus, no doubt drawing glasses on seraphim with Grandpa, his DNA was still flowing through my veins. After clearing my plan with Scott, my boys and I got to work. We found a big blown-down hemlock tree a few yards off of a snowshoe trail. We then dug out under the tree and surrounded the entryway with pine boughs.

The last and most important step was the placement of Zak's bear head. The bear head was a nasty-looking, snarling bear mount that my son had bought for five dollars at a garage sale. This head was carefully placed in the entrance of the den. All it needed now was just a few more pine boughs covering the entrance, and it was game on.

The day before the campers arrived, God blessed us with an additional eight inches of snow. The fresh snow covered up all evidence of our foul play. I love it when a plan comes together!

On Saturday we had about two dozen family campers signed up for the snowshoe nature hike. As we trekked along through the deep snow in the beautiful, rolling hardwood hills, we would pause occasionally to let people catch up as we shared some winter ecology facts.

As we crested a hill, I paused for a teachable moment. I explained to the group there was an active bear den just down the hill. The bear was hibernating, and we didn't want to wake it up. Everyone must be very quiet.

I explained, "I will go down first and peek in, just to make sure that it's safe. Then, one at a time, anyone who wants to can peek in. When you're done looking, just quietly back out."

I cautiously approached the den, knelt down, and parted the boughs. Then I quietly backed out, putting my finger to my lips, signaling the bear was there and they needed to be very quiet.

The first brave soul was a nine-year-old boy. I thought his eyes would fall out of his head as he hurried back up the trail, speechless.

The second one came back whispering, "I saw his teeth!"

Another kid said, "His eyes are open! We got to get out of here!"

Another one said, "I could smell his breath!"

Oh, what an imagination can do.

The grand finale was the best. She was, shall we say, a heavier-set, middle-aged woman. She was noticeably scared to death, but she did not want to be bested by her children. Now keep in mind the snow was about three feet deep and we were all in snowshoes on the side of a hill. The bear's open, snarling mouth was only about twelve inches behind the boughs.

Down on her hands and knees, she began to part the boughs. Instantly, with the grace and agility of an American ninja, she shot out of there, running backward up the hill. Leaping and doing a 180, she sprinted all the way back to camp!

With Scott and I rolling in the snow, her husband carefully evaluated the evidence. Sherlock then said, "There's not really a bear in there, is there?" Sorry, pal, but no, no there's not. You might want to go catch up with your wife though. At the rate she was moving, she'll be in Chicago within the hour!

One of my pranks actually came back to bite me. Keeping with the bear camp theme, I'll share one of my favorite stories. It happened during a summer family camp. Four or five families from our church were all camped back in a rustic area of camp. Several of us were enjoying an evening around the campfire telling stories and making S'mores.

Eventually someone noticed noises coming from the woods. These noises were in fact acorns dropping on dried leaves, but all they could think about was my earlier rebuke for discarding fish guts behind our campsite. These entrails not only smelled bad, but they could attract coons and bears into our camp site.

They concluded that the noises they were hearing just had to be a bear. With the stage set, I snuck off into my tent to change. I put on a black hat, sweatshirt, and jeans. As I crawled around the woods and berry brush, their conversations intensified. Certain it couldn't be a bear, Chuck, armed with a flashlight and a couple of kids, set out to see the bear. I was on all fours as I waited near some cover. When the flashlight finally shone in my direction, I darted into the berry brush. This quick glimpse sent the fearless explorers screaming back to the fire circle. Later, I casually walked back to the fire circle with some other adults to cover my tracks.

Later on, as it was getting late. Chuck decided to take our young visitors (about six kids) back to the main camp. With the stage set, I looked at my wife and said, "Can I?"

She smiled and said, "Go ahead."

With Chuck and the kids taking the long way back on the road, I raced across the country to get ahead of them. My shortcut took me through the woods and across the softball field. As I streaked (not literally) through the unlit infield, the joke was on me.

For you see, someone had pulled the foul ball net across from home plate to first base. I hit that net at full speed! Momentarily entangled, I swung out about ninety degrees before swinging back and getting launched, landing somewhere between the baseline and the pitcher's mound. I was lying flat on my back with the wind knocked out of me. I frantically searched for my glasses. I felt like Velma as I felt around the ground for my specs. Finally finding them, I then ran around the net and down the hill and hid in the ditch!

The berry brush in the ditch was the perfect ambush spot. The first of many streetlights was just around the corner, so it was now or never.

As I sat trying to catch my breath, my prey cautiously approached. I could hear them coming, their voices nervously chattering about bear attacks. They had flashlights in hand, fearfully shining them in every bush that could possibly contain a bear. Chuck was doing his best to reassure the kids that no bear was going to get them. That's when I leapt from the bushes with my best *rrrrrrrrarrr!*

Flashlights went airborne! Screams were deafening! Some ran in place while others ran to camp. Still others had their feet leave them as they fell to the ground. It could not have been any sweeter!

As I headed back to my campfire, I could hear the laughter growing louder and louder as the screaming grew distant. My wife had informed our posse of my intentions. Our camp mates had sat in silence awaiting the inevitable screams, which woke the whole camp! Chuck? Well, Chuck thought it was hilarious and forgave me soon after his heart rate returned to normal—although I'm not sure if the kids ever did.

Have you ever noticed people are often misguided in their attitudes and fears? They don't take the time to laugh, which, by the way, is a gift from God. More often they reason themselves into a panic rather than laughing at the ridiculousness of their situations.

Then our mouth was filled with laughter and our tongue with joyful shouting; "Then they said among the nations, The Lord has done great things for them." (Psalm 126:2)

God has done great things for us, including saving us from ourselves and our sins! Rejoice, live, love, and laugh! Life is way too short to spend it angry or a slave to irrational fears. Show the world that the joy of the Lord is your strength.

The fruit or evidence of the spirit in our lives is joy and peace. It's not fear and trembling. I believe one of the reasons Jesus chose the bunch of misfits he called disciples was simply because he loves to laugh. All of the crowds of children and adults that were drawn to Jesus were not drawn to a somber, judgmental lawgiver, someone waiting in the wings to jump all over them as soon as they messed up. But the crowds were drawn to a smiling, laughing, joy-filled teacher. I really doubt that he yelled when he taught. The only ones he ever publicly rebuked were the religious prudes.

Today, choose to smile and laugh.

Ponder this for a moment. How many times do you think the apostle John said to Peter, "Hey, it's the Lord!" just to watch Peter jump into the lake?

CHAPTER 22

Ground Shrinkage

Ground shrinkage is a sobering reality most of us will experience if we hunt or fish long enough. "That bass had to be eight pounds plus! I can't believe he broke my line! He would've been my best ever." Later that day your buddy lands that same fish and she tipped the scales at five pounds, two ounces. Your lure still embedded in her jaw. It's humbling to eat crow after you were sure it was much larger than it really was and you went on and on about it.

Or what about the massive bear you just arrowed? Surely you'll need to call all the neighbors to help you even roll it over! Then you walk up on it and you realize you could carry it out like a suitcase. Bears, I'll give you, are the most difficult to judge of any big game animals.

The more experience we have, the more accurate we become in judging trophies. We learn little tricks in estimating their age, sex, and score. Bears, for instance, have several telltale signs that give away their age, weight, and sex.

First off, males never travel with cubs. Males are also much broader at the shoulder than females, while females are much broader in the rump. Hmmm, does that sound vaguely familiar? The bigger a bear's ears look, the smaller or younger the bear is. They simply haven't grown into their ears yet, kind of like your neighbor kid. Likewise, that neighbor kid's teenage sibling is all legs and arms. Similarly, immature bears are gangly looking. Mature bears, on the other hand, have really filled out. Their bellies often hang so low they look as if they're dragging on the ground.

There are also good indicators available in estimating a buck's score. Deer vary greatly in size across the country. That said, I'll share the rule of thumb in my area of the Midwest. A whitetail buck's ears, on average, are about seven inches long. An alert buck that's facing you will measure sixteen to seventeen inches wide, ear tip to ear tip. A buck's eye is only about one inch in diameter, while the circular white hair around his eye is two to three inches in diameter. Most three-and-a-half-year-old bucks will score between 125 inches and 145 inches but will be lacking in antler mass. Often a four-and-a-half-year-old or older buck's burr or antler base will be as large as their eye patch. By knowing these few facts, you can usually judge an animal in the field. I say usually because there always seems to be an exception to the rule.

As far as ground shrinkage goes, my most embarrassing boast happened a few years ago. The last few days of early bow were winding down, and gun season was only five days away. The rut had slowed down to a crawl. I was perched in my platform stand, nestled in a narrow band of planted pines. The pines were four rows deep and about twenty feet high.

A twenty-foot pine simply will not adequately support any type of tree stand. Every time you break wind, you tend to pole vault back-and-forth! Fun, yes, but not conducive to good hunting. After several years of watching bucks pass just out of range as they traveled along the pines, it was time to improvise. A well-placed ground blind produced a nice nine-pointer that first year. The spot was definitely productive, but I hated the claustrophobic confinement of a ground blind.

The following spring I built a sixteen-foot, four-legged platform stand complete with a swivel seat. The three-by-five platform had garage sale Christmas trees sprouting up from each corner. Besides being festive, they helped to conceal my presence. The planted pines zigzagged along the edge of a cut cornfield. I placed the stand in the pines on the edge of a field road that split the pines. This bottleneck funneled the deer traveling east and west.

The only hang-up to this stand was that the ground was covered with grass and pine needles, making any approaching deer completely silent. The thick white pine cover also prevented me from seeing deer until they were literally standing in my shooting lanes. To sit here required a focused vigilance with bow in hand.

The beautiful morning I mentioned earlier produced four separate buck sightings. The largest was a respectable three-and-a-half-year-old eight-point. Tempting? Yes, but not what I had hoped for. The buck I had dreamed about was taken by a friend of mine a few weeks earlier.

The heavy, five-and-a-half-year-old "booner" sported eleven-inch brow tines and was appropriately named "twin towers." I had dreamed of that buck for the last two years. I even collected two of his sheds. But now he was off the hit list, and I had nothing to indicate the presence of another monster in the area. But history is quick to remind me, you just never know!

At 8:40 a.m., I looked at my cell phone to check the time. I had planned to sit until nine and then head off to work. Four bucks is a good morning hunt in anyone's books, and I had work to do. As I slid my phone back into my pocket, there he stood, ten yards away in between the pine rows. His massive antlers dwarfed his mature body. As he stepped forward under a pine, I raised and drew my bow. He was directly downwind of some golden estrus and heading straight for it. I had earlier placed the scent on the other side of the field road.

The buck stepped out on to the road and sniffed at the dipstick. My seventeen-yard shot was perfect on the quartering away buck. And to my amazement, he dropped in his tracks.

In utter disbelief, I leaned back in my seat as I thanked the Lord. I had to call Tony to share my joy. "Tony, I think I just shot my first booner! He's laying right there! I haven't even gotten down to

127

look at him yet. His antlers look huge! He has some trash points too. Wow! I am so pumped up! I have no idea what he'll score, but he's huge. I'll talk to you later. I have got to call Nick! There's no way I'll be able to get him into the back of the truck by myself. See ya!"

"Nick! Wake up." Nick was working nights at the time. "I just shot a monster and I need your help to get him into the truck! Get out to Bill's ASAP!"

After hanging up, I excitedly climbed down and approached my prize, but something didn't seem quite right? The antlers were indeed impressive—a beautiful, symmetrical, mainframe eight-pointer. He had matching split brow tines and matching flyers off his twelve-inch G2s. That's a twelve-pointer for those of you who struggle in math or a six-by-six for you westerners. He was certainly one of the coolest bucks I had ever laid my eyes on! His four nontypical points each had a perfect match on the opposite side.

But as big as he looked, he really wasn't that big. As I spread my fingers out between his main beams, his twenty-four-inch spread was quickly reduced to seventeen inches? His 180-inch rack. Well, it was also reduced by a few dozen inches. As I dragged my prize into the cornfield to begin the dirty work, my 200-pound buck dragged like a yearling.

An average three-and-a-half-year-old buck in our area field dresses out between 180 to 185 pounds. A four-and-a-half-year-old will usually go over 200 pounds. This buck was later aged at four and a half years old. His healthy but short little body field dressed out at a whopping 133 pounds! Talk about ground shrinkage! He kind of reminded me of Max, the Grinch's dog before the grinch trimmed Max's antlers down. Ahhh, sorry, Nick, for getting you out of bed. But while you're here, how about some pictures?

Try as we might, our first impressions are often wrong. They're often far from reality. When we don't take the time to study things, we can come to a rash perception or conclusion. From the moment I first saw that buck to the time he lay motionless was less than ten seconds. I had perceived his antlers as much larger because I didn't study his body or gather all the facts.

A few years prior to that hunt, I was sitting in a maple tree, located in a ravine about sixty yards behind the platform stand. It was October 20, and I had yet to even see a deer. But with the rut approaching, I was not worried. Things would surely begin to heat up soon.

As the sun started to touch the western horizon, I smashed my antlers together. *Click, click, grind, grind, break, click, click, grind, break!* I tossed in some grunts for good measure. Now I waited, grunting occasionally.

My typical rattling sequence will last no more than a minute and a half, with a fifteen to twenty-second break in the middle. A buck fight is more of a wrestling match than a boxing match, and your calling should mirror that. Grind a lot, click a little.

My stand faces the setting sun, and as I squinted into the sun's rays shining through the trees, I noticed movement. There he was—the first buck of the year. He stopped on a hill about thirty yards away, staring in my direction. He scanned the area for the delinquents that would dare trespass on his turf. My heart was in my throat at the year's first buck sighting!

After a careful study, I decided not to shoot him. He sported only a narrow, short-tined rack. His odd, nine-point rack went out wide and then straight forward. He kind of looked like Ferdinand the bull from the Looney Tunes cartoons. But the more I studied him, the more I waffled in my decision to let him pass. I had two buck tags in my pocket, so my season wouldn't be ending if I decided to shoot this buck. Besides, he looked physically mature even though his antlers were well inside his ears. With him in the freezer, it would really take the pressure off. If he gave me a good shot, I'd take him, I reasoned. Besides, the camera was rolling!

The buck slowly and cautiously made his way past me, looking up and staring at me on several occasions. At fourteen yards he was quartering away when he stopped to make a scrape. With his eyes closed, he rubbed his pre-orbital glands in an overhanging branch.

It was a perfect opportunity, so I raised my bow. The string came back smoothly as I anchored and settled my top pin behind his right shoulder. Thump! The buck crashed off. His short run only went about fifty yards and ended in the bottom of a ravine. His dirt nap was only about fifty yards from a field road on the other side of the ravine. This will be great, I thought. *An easy drag out.*

After I gathered Mark up for the recovery, I was shocked when it took the two of us over thirty minutes to drag him the short distance to the truck. Then we couldn't lift him into the back of my truck.

It seems his narrow, nine-point rack was actually nineteen and a half inches between the beams. I can't believe I came whisker close to letting that behemoth walk! When I hung him in the garage, with his legs spread wide and crammed against the ceiling, his head, neck, and shoulders still laid on the ground. His torso measured well over two feet longer than any other mature buck I had ever taken. To date, I have never seen a buck, alive or dead, come close to his immense size. So what did he weigh? No clue! Sorry, only the Lord knows.

The following week I did buy a scale, and I was blessed to use that scale a week or so later with my second buck tag. I put that tag on a 140-inch nine-point that field dressed at 185 pounds. His nose, by the way, hung twelve inches off the garage floor.

Ground shrinkage is when our eyes, hopes, and desires are confronted with reality. I was thrilled with both of those animals even though neither one measured up to my expectations, for better or worse.

Scripture tells us to be thankful or grateful for all things and in all situations. Your spouse may not be the gangly youth he or she once was. He or she may now even more closely resemble a grouchy old mature bear—but he or she is yours! You married your spouse for better or worse. Thank the Lord for him or her. The same goes for your job, your kids, as well as your country.

We have so much to be thankful for. All these areas I mentioned have, no doubt, experienced some type of ground shrinkage. But that doesn't change the blessings they truly are or how much they would be missed if they were suddenly taken away. God's desire from you is simply for your thankfulness.

Rejoice in the Lord always; and again I say rejoice! Let your gentle spirit be known to all men. The Lord is near. Be anxious for nothing, but in everything by prayer and supplication with thanksgiving let your requests be made known to God. And the peace of God, which surpasses all comprehension, will guard your hearts and minds in Christ Jesus. Finally, brethren, whatever is true, whatever is honorable, whatever is right, whatever is pure, whatever is of good repute, if there is any excellence and if anything worthy of praise, dwell on these things. (Philippians 4:4–8)

Take some time today and thank the Lord for all the blessings you may be taking for granted. They would surely be missed if they were suddenly taken away.

CHAPTER 23

Expectations

As I write this, hanging above my right shoulder is a beautiful whitetail deer mount. He watches over every move I make. He's only been so employed for a very short time. In fact, I just finished airbrushing him last night. Painting around his eyes, mouth, and nose and inside his ears and nostrils are critical to making a mount look alive or natural. That's the goal in taxidermy—to make admirers swear the animal just blinked or is about to flip back into the water.

The art of taxidermy requires many different skills. They include a trained eye for detail, a steady hand, as well as a creative mind. The most important skill one must possess, though, is patience. Patience is what ultimately will distinguish a bad mount from a good one. A lack of patience will cause your work to truly suffer. If you skip or rush over the details, your impatience will be on display forever.

As I study my mount, I realize it won't win any awards. It does look good but not great. My eyes are immediately drawn to my mistakes—mistakes that most onlookers would never even notice. For example, I can tell that I didn't put enough sculpting clay in the ear bases, so they are not filled out as much as I would've liked them to be. And if you look close, his right tear duct is slightly lower than his left.

I had great expectations of a perfect, lifelike mount. As the mount's great designer, I noticed every detail and every flaw that exempts him from my standard of perfection. To the casual observer, he looks great, but my eyes are immediately drawn to those two negatives.

Our expectations set the bar for our hunts as well as our lives. This past fall my expectations were set very high. They have to be! After all, if you shoot at nothing, you'll hit it every time. I had several weeks set aside to hunt in Montana with my wife and son. With my Wisconsin bear tag filled, it was now time to punch my elk and deer tags.

Our first afternoon in Montana found Mark and me in a familiar basin. Earlier in the season Mark had several encounters here with some truly awesome bucks. The basin had also been filled with screaming bulls. Tonight was different, though, as not a single bugle could be heard. Numerous other hunters were also around, patrolling the area. But the worst expectation killers were the three grizzlies that were sharing our space. It really makes it hard to relax and enjoy a hunt when you're always watching your backside.

As we hiked out of the basin that evening, I spotted a nice mule deer buck. He certainly wasn't huge but a nice three-year-old nonetheless. I figured that if I could get within bow range, I'd take him. I made it to bow range just as shooting light was fading. With the buck standing broadside, it was now or never. But just as I raised my bow, the buck spooked.

I turned to see Mark walking up behind me, saying, "Don't shoot him, Dad. You can do a lot better than him. After all, it's only the first day!" He was very confident as he reassured me to hold off. For the record, I ended up eating my mule deer tag that year! Kids, sigh …

When I go out hunting, I do expect to see and harvest a deer, bear, bull … whatever! After all, optimism and expectation are the very things that fuel our drive. If you don't expect good things to happen, they won't. Usually it's because you won't put in the necessary effort to make good things happen. Try as I might, I never did fill that deer tag. I passed up numerous does and smaller bucks but only saw one true shooter, and we were unable to close the gap on him.

After hiking back to the truck that first night, our optimism had taken a direct hit. Between the hunting pressure, grizzlies, numerous wolf tracks, and all remaining elk giving us the silent treatment it was time to move on to plan B.

After discussing our options, we decided plan B would be a different area about a three-hour drive away. It was on the other side of the highway, and hopefully it held fewer hunters and supposedly no grizzlies. After a short night, the next day's efforts only produced two cows and a few deer.

We continued to hunt this area for a few more days before deciding to jump ship again. Although moose sightings abounded, elk sign was sparse.

After we picked up my wife, we set up camp in yet another new area but were sadly met with similar results. We found the majority of the elk had been pushed down onto the private lands earlier in the season and there was little to no bugling on the public lands.

After two weeks of hard hunting, all we had to show for our efforts was a buck that Mark had arrowed. Sometimes it's hard to keep optimistic or expectant when you're exhausted and you're not seeing any game. But that's when our faith really has to be strong. History has proven that despite the circumstances, I'll eventually get at least one good opportunity at a bull. I prayed and asked for that opportunity.

Truth be told, elk or no elk, I was having a blast with my family. Mark and I shot countless mountain grouse with our bows as we burned boot leather through some of the most incredible scenery in the world. My wife was with us in spirit as she enjoyed her quiet time back in camp. At noon she and I would hike the fire trails hand in hand, enjoying God's beautiful creation. It was awesome! Getting a bull or even seeing one would be just icing on the cake.

Eventually our travels brought us back to where we saw the two cows on the second day. We were hoping that some elk had moved into the area. And if nothing else, that area held quite a few mule deer.

Our first night back, we hiked to the top of a mountain overlooking several basins. Our plan was to glass and call, in hopes of locating a bull for the next morning. We sat glassing a large opening on an adjacent mountain a mile or so away. The opening was covered with sporadic blow downs and jack pines. We sat and talked while we listened for bugles. After a while, I spotted an elk. This elk grew a nice six-by-six rack as I watched him. I described the location to Mark, and he soon spotted the elk.

"That's only a rag horn," he said.

I replied, "No, it's a nice bull!"

"No, it's a rag horn!"

Back and forth we bantered until eventually the two bulls stood next to each other. Hmm, I guess we were both right.

"What are we waiting for? We still have about forty-five minutes until dark. Let's go get them!"

Those were the first bulls we had seen in two weeks of hard hunting. The animals were at least a mile away as the crow flies, and we were on top of a relatively open but very steep mountain. The elk were down the mountain, across the creek, and about three hundred yards up the other side.

Now, just to be clear, if this was a herd we had spotted, we would have formulated a game plan for the next day. But two bachelor bulls could wander miles from there by morning, so it was game on. It was now or never! My knees screamed from the jarring as we ran down the side of that steep slope. We were trying our best to keep our balance as we raced against the clock.

As we neared the bottom, Mark said, "Wow, look at the size of that grizzly scat!"

It was the size of a cow flop, swollen from the rain. And it was really fresh! "Don't worry about it," I said. "We've got to keep going or we'll run out of daylight."

Fifty yards later I looked up and spotted a big bear just across the creek. He was very dark and facing away from us about sixty yards out. He was also directly in our line of travel. He was feeding behind a big pine, which prevented us from getting a good look at him.

Mark was holding a black bear tag and wanted to sneak in for a better look. I stayed put as Mark closed the distance from sixty, fifty, forty, down to thirty yards. The bear would occasionally glance over his shoulder. I in turn would pace back and forth on the open hillside. This allowed the bear to see what he was most likely smelling. We didn't want any trouble with this bear, but he was directly between us and the elk. The surrounding terrain was all rock cliffs, making it nearly impossible to go around him. At thirty yards the bear stepped out and gave Mark the view he needed. His big, dished-out face, long claws, and a big hump on his shoulder left us with no doubts.

Nuts! We couldn't shoot him. That huge bear was in fact a six to seven hundred–pound grizzly! I was armed with a can of bear spray in one hand and my pistol in the other. I noisily walked toward Mark, while the bear, much to our relief, disappeared up the hill.

Mark and I still had a couple of hundred yards to cover before we reached the jack pines, and darkness was closing in quickly. Our hurried pace slowed as we approached the opening. Peeking in and seeing nothing, I cautiously snuck up to the area we had last seen the bulls. I went as far as I dared and chose to stand in an open area on a knob next to a couple of six-foot jack pines. Mark stayed about sixty yards behind me and started to cow call. I joined in, and before long, I heard elk coming.

Straight out in front of me, the smaller bull crested a small ridge. The five-by-five stopped and was facing me at forty yards. He would go no further until he could set his eyes on one of those mouthy cows. There was not one twig between us, but with him facing and staring directly at me, there was no possibility of shot. All I could do was wait and pray.

After a few minutes, I heard another elk approaching. I'll never forget that majestic six-by-six rack drifting over that ridge. The second bull stopped directly behind the first one. Now I had two sets of eyes staring in my direction. There's no way I could draw my bow without getting spotted, and neither bull was offering me a shot. As Mark let out his best seductive cow calls, I prayed for one of the bulls to turn broadside.

The first bull finally cooperated. He was nervous and about to depart when he turned and stopped, quartering away as I drew back. I settled my forty-yard pin on the center of his chest. Anchor point? Check! Forty-yard pin? Check! Pick a spot? Check! Stabilize? Check! Squeeze the trigger! Twang! My expectations instantly turned to dismay. I watched my arrow fly true, only then to plane upward as it sailed over the closer bull's back. Both bulls disappeared as they crashed off through the blow downs.

Mark came up to me super excited, expecting a long pack out, complete with tenderloins for supper. His optimism continued as I relayed my story. As we searched for my arrow, we could hear the elk in the distance barking out their displeasure!

The next morning we quickly recovered my arrow. That day was filled with a combination of disappointment and relief. Disappointed that I didn't harvest the bull and that I had somehow missed, but relieved the bull was running around still looking for love. We were also very relieved that the grizzly did not come after us or the bull.

To this day I'm still not sure why my arrow planed that way. I was using a new, large, expandable-type broadhead. Some friends speculated that it had opened prematurely. I'll never know for sure. Thankfully, the night before we left for home God blessed me with a fat cow for the freezer.

My expectations for that fall were only partially met. Driving home with the trophy racks strapped to my truck never materialized, while the memories and great times with my wife and son will never be forgotten. The expectation of a full freezer did happen. Safety during a season filled with multiple grizzly encounters was thankfully realized. The expectation of next year? Well, that's in process!

Delight yourself in the Lord and he will give you the desires of your heart. (Psalm 37:4)

I'm still waiting for my desired big bull. But I've learned to delight myself with the Lord as I walk each day with him. He is with me through every sunrise and sunset and every moment in between.

Abraham waited fourteen years for the son God had promised him. In those fourteen years, God greatly prospered Abraham. I have been greatly blessed with many great memories and experiences as I wait upon the Lord. We only have to look at our blessings as we wait on the Lord to fully enjoy the whole of our expectations.

What are you believing God for? Try not to be so focused on the prize that you miss out on the many blessings along the way.

CHAPTER 24

Mistaken Identity

Many years ago, I learned a very valuable lesson. The lesson is that it's impossible to out-give God. Twenty years ago I left a good job, a job I really enjoyed, to go into full-time ministry. Strangely enough, it wasn't my home, job, or financial security that I struggled with leaving. It was the false belief that I could never again hunt out west. A missionary's income is solely based on what people give them. I was on missionary staff at a north woods Christian camp. How could I possibly justify a $1,000 elk tag, especially when I might only receive $800 a month for my family to live off of?

Still, I was believing God would meet our needs, and he didn't disappoint. We lived off of a lot of venison in those days, but I can honestly say we never missed a meal. Somehow, God always provided enough that our bills were also always paid on time.

One of the little details or concerns I had was God's ability or provision in fulfilling my desire to hunt. God not only cared about my desires, but gave me some serious accommodation upgrades. Over the course of time, hunters tend to find each other. Well, I was no exception to the rule, as God faithfully led me to some new friends.

One year my new friends invited me to join them on their annual elk hunt in the Missouri breaks. Jim just happened to own a comfortable, air-conditioned cabin located in the breaks. All of my previous elk hunts involved a tent pitched on public land. Awesome upgrade! Thanks, Lord!

This new area also held elk—lots of big elk! One particular morning, I watched a bachelor group of eleven bulls. The smallest bull was a nice five-by-five, and the two largest bulls were both over 380 inches. I had never witnessed anything like it, before or since.

By the way, on this hunt, I was just along for the ride. Well, I was also along to do the calling and to pack out the meat. Hmmm, come to think about it, I guess I was actually their mule. The closest thing to a bow I was carrying was the string on my bugle tube.

Our evenings were spent in the high country calling to bedded bulls or sitting over water holes. Our mornings were really a chess match, as we hoped to be sitting on the right exit trail. The elk would feed all night in the corn and hayfields and then head back up to their beds at dawn. Sitting on the right trail was often just a game of chance. Over the course of the week, we would narrow down the most frequented crossings as we hoped for the best.

After taking into consideration the predominant winds, we dug a foxhole for Tony to sit in. Sagebrush being our only available cover. Tony had dug in about twenty yards north of a heavily used game trail, while I was stationed on a ridge only a few hundred yards east of his position.

With the star-studded sky starting to lighten, we could hear numerous bulls screaming back and forth at each other in the valley. Hopefully today was the day. Although Tony had many close encounters over the years, he had yet to harvest a bull with his bow. Our expectations were pretty high as we prayed that today would be the day.

With the cow decoy silhouetted against the eastern skyline, I let out some cow calls. I soon noticed a nice bull and cow emerge over Tony's ridge a mere twenty yards away from him.

Thawap! Tony's arrow hit home! The bull raced into the valley between us, making a little semicircle before collapsing. Like a PBR bull rider, he went from first kick to dirt nap in eight seconds. The bull was down. I was elated! I jumped around excitedly, trying desperately to hold my composure.

Tony, on the other hand, oddly enough, held his position. Like Her Majesty's royal guard, he stood motionless. After a few minutes, I walked down to the bull. He was a big, beautiful six-by-five, and I was thrilled. When I started to walk up to Tony, he trotted down to me.

"How big is he?"

"A six-by-five," I replied.

Tony came unglued! He gave me a monster bear hug as he jumped around excitedly, while telling me his story.

Apparently, a huge buck pushing thirty inches wide was following the elk. Tony thought for a minute he just might get a double. But when the elk ran off, the buck doubled back. It was now time to check out his bull.

Many years of hopes, dreams, and desires were fulfilled in that moment. That bull was everything Tony had dreamed of, and I was blessed to have shared the experience with him. Tony had made it possible for me to come along, and we were both incredibly blessed by his generosity. Tony had his best elk hunt ever. And I got to enjoy the first of many more trips west. Both of us also received a really good friend and lifelong hunting partner that week. God really does have your best interests in mind. He does care about what's important to you. Yes, even elk hunting! You can never out-give him.

Tony's friendship was not the only one I forged on that trip. Jim, the cabin's owner, and I also developed a close friendship. It grew close enough that after a few more good trips, Jim and I decided it was time for a couples' hunt.

The four of us excitedly made our plans. Carol, Jim's wife, had joined us on some previous hunts. But how were these two women going to get along for a week alone in a cabin?

Living at opposite ends of the state, our wives had only met for supper once before the big trip arrived. But like heaven and hell, how we spend our time is our choice. For the record, the girls became very close friends. Both of our wives are devout believers, and they spent their days in praise and worship. They also enjoyed some long hikes and jigsaw puzzles.

Neither of our wives are hunters, and since Jim didn't draw a tag that year, that left only me carrying a bow on this trip. Long before first light, Jim and I would hike out to our designated spots. Jim would sit on a high ridge glassing for movement while he enjoyed the incredible views. I was stationed at the end of a steep washout.

The washout was about twenty feet deep and straight down. It was well over a hundred yards long, forcing all game to go around it. I had dug out a place to sit at the very end of the south side of the washout. Sitting between two sage bushes, I was very well concealed, with the predominant morning winds blowing my scent out over the washout.

That first morning found me excitedly waiting for first light. I was watching the stars fade as I listened to the distant bulls bugling their challenges. I was also anxiously anticipating my first game sighting and was not disappointed. Although no elk had made an appearance, I was able to watch a lot of mule deer. One string of about twelve mule deer took the trail around the opposite side of the washout. With my binoculars, I inspected each animal. Six wore antlers, but most were small. There was also one decent buck in the group. Then there was one old buck that was just plain goofy looking. I'm not sure if even his mother could love that rack.

About a half hour later, my heart rate leaped as I watched a pair of shooters crest the ridge by Tony's old foxhole. Nuts! They were well out of range and offered no opportunity for a stalk. The first buck was a huge, unique-looking, heavy fork. His antlers resembled goal posts. All of his tines were pointing straight up at the sky. His antlers were incredibly tall and thick. He was a unique trophy for sure.

His partner was no slouch either—a wide three-by-four that was at least twenty-eight inches inside. An awesome buck to say the least, but my heart was set on that big fork.

The next morning found me in the same location. The first deer to move through were a couple of does. They walked up the same trail they had the previous day. Next came some little bucks. The forks and three pointers fed by me at a mere twenty yards. They were joined by a slightly bigger four-by-four. All four of these bucks had stopped and were browsing within twenty yards of me. This is why I love bowhunting. Having four bucks that close, at eye level, is well worth the price of admission.

The four-by-four was tempting, but he was only a two-and-a-half-year-old. Besides, my heart was set on that monster fork. As I sat motionless, watching the show, I caught movement back to the right. I slowly turned my head and saw the big three-by-four coming down the ridge. There was also another, bigger deer in front of him.

They were headed down the same trail the four smaller bucks had just taken. I had previously mentally marked out different ranges and knew the bucks were all well within bow range. I was forced to look through a big sage bush once the deer came farther down the slope. With the wind starting to swirl and all those eyes around, I knew I had to act soon.

I waited until the four feeding bucks were all looking away and drew my bow. I slowly eased my bow around the bush until I could see the bigger deer's body. Picking a spot, I released and watched my arrow hit its mark! The deer raced off to the south as the other five bucks scattered for parts unknown.

After a half-hour wait, I took up the trail. I quickly found my buck as he only went about eighty yards. As I approached him, my emotions went from elation to dismay. "You have got to be kidding!" I loudly exclaimed.

Lying before me was arguably the ugliest buck I have ever seen. His right antler was indeed a big fork while his left one resembled a man's hand. It not only looked like a hand, but it also was literally no bigger than one. He had a massive old body, which was all I could see through the sage bush. His body was much bigger than any of the other bucks within sight. His physical size coupled with the presence of his three-by-four traveling companion tricked me into believing he was the big fork.

All of our lives, we are told to stay calm, pick a spot, and don't look at the antlers! Can I just go on record by saying, look at the antlers!

It was obvious this old boy didn't have enough chlorine in his gene pool. When I first saw him the day before. I remember thinking, Boy, I couldn't imagine ever shooting him. I guess never say never!

I admit, I was more than a little disappointed with my trophy at first. I had been dreaming of big bucks and bulls for the past nine months. I passed up a truly impressive three-by-four while shooting a buck everyone laughs at. Although he wasn't the beautiful trophy buck I dreamed of, he ate great, and he was still a mature mule deer buck harvested with a bow. It's been said that beauty is in the eye of the beholder, and I believe a trophy is too.

Later that week, I managed to shoot a herd bull out of that exact same spot. Okay, he was only a spike, but technically he was the only bull in a herd of nine cows. Therefore, herd bull! About a year later, I discovered while watching some hunting show that some blond named Tiffany actually shot the true herd bull, a big six-by-six. I can only assume they busted the rest of the herd over to me during the recovery. So thanks, Blondie. They were the only elk we saw all week.

I entitled this chapter "Mistaken Identity." The buck I shot was not the buck I thought he was. His funky antlers made him less than desirable in our eyes. Too often we look on outward appearances rather than what's inside. We fixate on some negative aspects rather than the whole.

But the Lord said to Samuel, "Do not look at his appearance or at the height of his stature, because I have rejected him; for God sees not as man sees, for man looks at the outward appearance, but the Lord looks at the heart." (1 Samuel 16:7)

That buck most likely had a previous injury that resulted in his undesirable appearance.

Sometimes people look and act the way they do because of previous injuries. These could be either physical or emotional. I renamed my ugliest buck ever "the stud" because of his two-by-four rack. God renamed those who believe in His son Jesus, sons, daughters, adopted, children of the king, chosen, elect, redeemed, forgiven, beloved, justified, and victorious overcomers! Those sure sound a lot better than ugly, orphan, loser, or anything else man may call you. Who are you going to believe, man or God?

God is a God of truth! Believe in who you are in Christ and what God says about you. That is your true identity and destiny. Keep your chin up and walk in a manner worthy of your calling!

CHAPTER 25

Trophies

One of the highlights of my year is the annual Wisconsin deer and turkey expo. The expo is held about a half hour north of my house on the first weekend of April. It's a great excuse for friends and relatives from around the state to come down and join me for the weekend.

We spend our time swapping new stories and reliving some timeless classics. We hike around the rolling hills, looking for sheds as we scout for new stand locations. I usually take advantage of their presence by recruiting them to help me move or set up a few new deer stands.

All the buck sign from the previous fall is still around. And a good spot last year will most likely be a good spot this year. I'm a firm believer in doing all of your woods work in the spring. I believe the only scouting you should be doing in the fall is what you happen to see on the way to your stands or cameras. The more you traipse around in the fall, the more evidence you will leave behind for a wary buck to find.

Saturday morning, after a hearty breakfast, we all head off to the expo. Hundreds of vendors are there, eagerly showing off all the latest and greatest gadgets. They boast that these gadgets will almost guarantee you a monster buck, bull, or bear this fall. The way they talk, you would have sworn that no trophies had ever been harvested prior to their invention hitting the market. All other broadheads, arrows, rests, releases, scent control, camo, etc., were obviously inferiorly made by "Ugh" in a cave!

There are also aisle after aisle of outfitters from around the world with huge trophy mounts looking over their shoulders and trophy-laden photo albums spread out in front of them. Our eyes lit up as we dream of ourselves smiling with one of those bucket list animals.

The outfitter would grin and say, "I still have two openings left for this fall!"

We would reluctantly ask, "How much?"

With a firm grip on reality, we politely thanked them for their time as we walked away. We contemplated the exchange of six months' salary for a weeklong hunt. Hmm. *Maybe I'll just buy a hunting video instead. After all, videos are a lot cheaper than divorce court!*

My favorite part of the expo is looking, gawking, lusting, dreaming, desiring, wishing, hoping, and fantasizing as I drool over all the monster bucks. Besides the vendors' mounts, the Wisconsin DNR is there with the wall of shame. The wall of shame is a display of twenty to thirty trophy bucks. These monster bucks were confiscated by the DNR because they were harvested illegally. What a waste!

The grand finale for us is the boardwalk. With many official scorers on hand, hunters are encouraged to bring in their trophies for measuring. Along with their score sheets, the bucks are then displayed for all of us gawkers to admire. Hundreds of trophies, ranging from world records and 200-inch monsters, to "What could they possibly be thinking?" line the walls.

All the bucks displayed were harvested in Wisconsin over the past few years. They were harvested by a variety of means, including archery, firearms, muzzleloaders, Chevys, Fords, and Dodges, all proudly displayed for us to enjoy. We all leave the expo dreaming of the upcoming hunting season, which is now only six months away. We then hurry home, anxious to try out all of our new gadgets.

God has blessed me with numerous trophies of my own over the years, but one really sticks out. That buck in particular was the climax of a three-year pursuit.

I was hunting in north-central Wisconsin with my dad. Dad was sitting/sleeping with his recurve at the tip of a swamp. I was set up a couple hundred yards south of him. I had chosen a maple tree that was about thirty yards off of a poplar slashing. The thick poplars were about two inches in diameter. A heavy game trail paralleled the slashing, and I was set up downwind of its intersection with another trail.

The afternoon was perfect, dead calm, and slightly overcast, with forty-degree temps. It was November 3, and the rut was just cranking up. A monster fourteen-pointer roamed these woods, and today, well it just felt right! After putting out some Tinks 69, I eased my climber up the tree and settled in about twenty feet up.

That fourteen-pointer was huge, and he had it all: height, width and mass. I was fantasizing about him when I heard the distinct sound of hooves in the leaves.

Eventually the deer made its appearance, cautiously working his way down the game trail. The setting suns final rays glistened off of his antlers. He was on the trail paralleling the poplars and heading in my direction. The doe in heat scent definitely had his attention! He was being drawn in, like a bass lure. I thought, This just might work! as I mentally prepared for a shot.

I had waited my whole life for this one opportunity, and now it looked as if it would finally happen. I had spent countless hours practicing, scouting, and dreaming. Now with my heart in my throat and my knees wobbling, I drew back and placed the thirty-yard site pin behind his left shoulder.

I held my breath and squeezed the trigger on my release. Twang! The arrow was off in a flash. Zing! The trailing string whirled from its spool. The buck jumped and crashed off as the string sputtered to a stop.

I could hear the buck crashing through the poplars, but the string just blew in the breeze. Did I miss? I would have sworn that I had drilled him. The deer was still moving, but the flipping string wasn't! My thoughts raced back and forth.

As the lengthening shadows gave way to darkness, I climbed down to retrieve my arrow. It shouldn't be hard to find, I reasoned. After all, all I had to do was follow the string, right? The string led me to a thick patch of berry brush. With the string broken and wrapped around the thorny briars, I was left to ponder, *Did I hit him or not? Did I shoot in front of him and he just dragged the string with him?* My mind raced with way too many questions and no answers.

I retrieved my climber and met up with Dad. After a closer investigation, we were unable to locate my arrow or any blood with our less-than-stellar flashlights. It was forecast to drop into the low twenties that night, so I wasn't worried about meat spoilage. We decided it was best to just return in the morning.

A heavy frost greeted us as we made our way through the crisp autumn woods. I had hardly slept a wink that night as I wondered what we would find. But the cold, fresh air had awakened all my senses as we searched for my arrow. The search ended quickly, as Dad found my arrow just past where the buck had initially stood. It was covered with bright red, frozen crystals. My shot was a complete pass-through! There was about ten feet of string still attached to the arrow. So much for that gadget being the godsend it was advertised to be!

We slowly followed the game trail the buck had taken into the thick poplars. With the sparse drops of blood concealed by the heavy frost, our best bet was to just keep following the game trail. There were long gaps between drops of blood, and I was really concerned.

As I searched for the next drop, Dad said, "There he is!"

Thrilled, I started hugging and arm punching my dad. I was elated! Reaching down, I grabbed the buck's rack and started counting the points. One, two—yup, that's it! A massive three-inch spiker. My very first deer with a bow! I could not have been happier or more excited.

I had hardly dreamed of much else over the last three years. I finally got a buck with a bow! I had been bowhunting behind our house daily since I was twelve, jumping at every opportunity I was given to try new places. Now at fifteen, I had accomplished my life long goal. My trophy was down! And the best part was, my dad was there with me.

All the misses and close calls over the last three years just made my success even sweeter. The monster fourteen-pointer would just have to wait until next year. My little eleven-pointer would just have to do for now.

The joy I felt that day and the sense of accomplishment is why I hunt. It's not about killing; it's about accomplishing a goal. That's what trophies are given out for. Somebody accomplished a feat that others weren't able to. The Super Bowl, the Masters, the World Series, no matter what the sport, a trophy awaits the victor. While missed opportunities haunt the runner-up.

As hunters, we don't compete against other hunters. We compete against our quarry. A deer's ears can hear seven times better than ours. Their eyesight ranges out to 280° where ours is limited to less than 160°. Their sense of smell can reach out to miles, while ours is limited to feet. To beat an animal's eyes, ears, and noses with archery equipment, all while sitting in their living room, is a true accomplishment.

Too often we put too much emphasis on the size of a trophy's antlers rather than the entire experience of the harvest. I'm guilty of this too. As I walk down the expo hallway admiring the huge whitetails Wisconsin has produced, I have to remind myself when I see someone proudly displaying their eighty-inch eight-point that it's their trophy of a lifetime. They couldn't be happier or more proud. They accomplished their goal.

The joy is truly in the journey. The joy is in the challenge, the adventures, and the people you share it with. A trophy on the wall is only a reminder of that journey. Your priceless shoulder mount will eventually be lucky to sell for a hundred bucks on craigslist simply because only you have the memories associated with it.

I love football. I enjoy watching as thirty-two hopeful teams pursue the Lombardi trophy. Yet only one accomplishes its goal. With few exceptions (I won't name names here Lions fans), most teams will win at least a few games each year. Those few games may be the highlight of their season. Most players will never reach the Super Bowl throughout their entire careers. Was their time wasted? Do they regret playing the game? Hardly! They spent their time getting paid to compete in a game that they loved. As sportsmen, we compete in a game we love.

Enjoy the journey, my friends, keeping your eyes on the true prize of the upward call of Christ Jesus. Don't lose sight of the joy in the journey. Lofty goals can inspire us to greatness, but they can also distract us from what's really important. Take the time to evaluate your goals and journeys today.

Personally, I would define a trophy as any animal that will make you happy!

CHAPTER 26

Let 'Em Go, Let 'Em Grow

I sat motionless, nervously waiting for the buck to turn his head. Years of experience, trials, and errors had taught me that if you can see a deer's eyes, it can see you! Humans were created to be predators. Our eyes, like other predators, are located on the front of our heads. Dogs, cats, wolves, foxes, bears, mountain lions, etc., all have their eyes located on the front of their heads. They were designed to focus in on their prey.

On the other hand, prey animals, otherwise known as herbivores or salad eaters, have eyes on the sides and tops of their heads. This gives them about a 280° sight picture, allowing them to detect danger from above as well as around, without ever having to turn their heads. Rabbits, deer, elk, moose, turkeys, etc., are all equipped with these upper side-mounted optics.

All the fancy camo in the world will not hide you if a deer catches you moving. The best rule of thumb is never move when you can see their eyes.

The buck was moving toward me from the north. He was a young, wide eight-pointer, a three-and-a-half-year-old with a ton of potential. He was sporting a very distinctive rack. It measured at least twenty inches inside. He's a buck I would have passed on a week earlier, but now bow season was winding down and gun season was only two days away.

Just yesterday, that same buck came by me shortly after daybreak. Walking up from my right, he stopped a mere twenty yards away. I slowly raised my bow as I swiveled my body into position. The buck had been quartering away, but he still managed to see that slight movement. Busted! He snapped his head up and glared in my direction. Unsure of what he had seen, he trotted off and stopped about fifty yards away.

I tried unsuccessfully to lure him back into bow range with different grunts and bleats. Unimpressed, he eventually continued on his mission of finding a girlfriend.

Now that same buck was again heading my way as he worked his way along the ridge. If he stayed the course, he would pass slightly behind me and to my left. My prayers were soon answered as he stopped in the crusty snow seventeen yards away. With his head behind a bush, I drew back undetected. With the buck positioned over my left shoulder, I was forced to contort myself around the double wide ladder stand's seat.

I picked a spot and squeezed the release. Bang! My bow lurched downward as my lower limb slapped the stand's seat. This unexpected impact sent my arrow low and to the right, barely grazing his belly. The buck raced up the valley and stopped at the edge of the cut corn field. He stared back at me for several minutes before eventually trotting off across the field. I was devastated. Two opportunities in two days and I blew them both! Sometimes you just have to wonder if it just isn't meant to be.

Two years later, I was perched in my platform stand. It was a perfect November 4th morning, cold and calm. Tony was down for the weekend, and I was sure at any moment a bruiser would pass by one of us.

A quick glance at my phone made my heart skip a beat. Scott had texted, saying he had just shot a beast. Awesome! A buck down and we were only a half hour into the day. Scott was hunting on his property ten miles away—the same property I had missed the big eight-pointer on two years earlier. As we texted back and forth, we decided to meet up at 11:00 a.m. Scott would definitely need help with this recovery.

I had never seen Scott so excited as he shared his story! As Scott walked into his stand that morning, he sprayed some buck bomb around, hoping to lure in a passing buck. He climbed into his stand and started praying. He was frustrated, as he hadn't even seen a buck yet that season. He opened his eyes to see the bruiser buck standing at the base of his tree. The buck was sniffing curiously at the foliage. Scott somehow managed to draw and shoot while the buck was preoccupied with the scent of his dream girl!

Thwhack! His perfect shot sent the buck charging off across the creek bottom and collapsing at the base of the hill. Scott had recovered the buck and field dressed him before Tony and I had arrived.

I was awestruck to say the least. The three-and-a-half-year-old eight-point that had given me the slip, had matured into a truly magnificent animal. The eighteen-pointer grossed 193 Boone and Crockett inches! It boasted a twenty-six-and-a-half-inch inside spread. And it took all three of us to drag his massive body up and out of that steep ravine.

The only negative to the hunt was his right main beam was broken off about halfway out. Thankfully, a taxidermist working off trail cam photos was able to reconstruct the missing bone. The buck was a jaw-dropping buck of a lifetime for Scott or any bowhunter, for that matter. I still can't help but wonder what the buck looked like that busted him up.

I admittedly was a little frustrated when I missed him two years earlier. But I do remember thinking, *Maybe some kid will get him or maybe he'll survive and I'll get a crack at him next year.* Now two years later, I was grunting and groaning as I pulled him up a steep bank through a briar patch. Scott was next to me, grinning like he'd just won the lottery.

I guess a big kid did get him after all! As I struggled up that hill I couldn't help but think, *What if I had made the shot? What if I had harvested that buck two years earlier? This moment would have never happened. Scott's desire for a booner would have been left unfulfilled.*

Most of us have heard of the "let 'em go, let 'em grow" catchphrase of the quality deer management program (QDMA). It basically promotes the philosophy of giving bucks a chance to reach their potential by not shooting them when they're immature.

I am a firm believer in QDMA and what it accomplishes. Most bucks will just start to crack the door open on their potential when they are three and a half years old. A three-and-a-half-year-old buck can be a very tempting target. In southern Wisconsin, most three-and-a-half-year-old bucks will score around 130 inches. In many parts of our great country, a 130-incher will get your picture in the paper.

I remember a few years back passing on a three-and-a-half-year-old eight. He had incredibly long brow times, but it was still early in the rut as he chased a doe past me. They both stopped just down the hill from my stand. I had a dilemma. He was a nice buck and was standing in the open, only twenty-five yards away. I decided to let him go so he could grow. It just happened to be the same season that I later ate my tag after missing the wide eight point.

Hmmm, mistake? Not at all! No regrets at all. I was blessed with the privilege of finding his long brow tined sheds later that spring. Then I watched him on camera as he grew into a dandy nine-pointer. Somehow he managed to avoid my stands that fall, all the while staying very photogenic.

The following spring, the neighbor found his sheds. I spent all summer and fall patterning him. His rack was now a massive Boone and Crockett candidate. On October 21, I received a text message with a picture of my friend with the great beast.

My sincere congratulations went out to Terry. Another buck of a lifetime went to a smiling, dedicated hunter. Later, I dropped off my set of his sheds so Terry's series could be complete.

Terry hunts hard, and he also had been patterning, watching, and dreaming of harvesting "twin towers" as he called him.

So why didn't I get one of those bucks? I have worked hard for a booner too. Is it just not meant to be? Hunting is kind of a microcosm of life.

Scripture tells us in Proverbs 16:9 that the mind of a man plans his way, but the Lord directs his steps. Verse 3 says, "Commit your works to the Lord and your plans will be established."

People often disagree on God's control over our lives. Some believe we are just puppets on his big stage. I personally believe God has a specific plan for each of our lives. But the only way his will or plan for our lives is accomplished is when we submit to it and actually do his will.

God is a good God. He doesn't rape, murder, or abuse children. He is the prince of peace. It's the devil that comes to kill, steal, and destroy! Jesus came to give us life and life abundantly (John 10:10). It's humans who do evil things when they don't obey or follow God's perfect will for their lives. God has given us free will to choose him or reject him, as well as rejecting his plan for our lives.

Romans 8:28 says, "God works all things for good to those who love God." This well-known and often-quoted verse simply doesn't apply to most people. Because, truth be told, most people don't love God! Most people actually hate God, often because they wrongly believe that God did something to them or to their loved one for some greater purpose.

What God did promise was that he would work out for good the plans, lives, and situations of those who do love him. It doesn't matter if you are responsible for your problem or someone else is. God will work it out for good when you trust Him and ask him to do it.

My 2016 season was filled with highs and lows. The Boone and Crockett bucks I dreamed of were harvested by friends. I was blessed with seeing their dreams come true and thrilled to have had a small part in it. My choices as well as my mistakes did affect others.

Later that season, God blessed me with my best buck to date. Amazingly enough, I didn't even know that buck existed. No doubt he was targeted by other hunters. Their choices to pass on him in previous years or possibly their mistakes or misses unknowingly became a great blessing to me.

May your choices and actions be a blessing to others today.

CHAPTER 27

Above Reproach

The big buck was a regular at the hayfield. Tony had numerous pictures of him. Sadly, most of those photos were taken well after dark. Tony was hopeful that the upcoming rut would cause the buck's love for the ladies to override his caution.

There were several decent bucks in the area, but this particular buck was the one that filled Tony's dreams. Every time we would talk, the conversation would soon turn to this shooter buck. Tony certainly had his heart set on him.

One morning Tony called, and his demeanor was different—so different, in fact, that I thought someone had died! "What's wrong?" I asked.

"Oh, it's terrible! Just terrible!" He went on to explain.

There was a new competition between some of the local high schools. The competition wasn't in football, hockey, or basketball. It was in poaching! These high schoolers had a contest to see who could poach the most and biggest deer. It involved high schools from several local counties. Their "rules" required bucks to be decapitated as proof of harvest. Does, after a quick picture, could be just left in the field to rot. These brilliant minds were keeping their contest's tally on Facebook. Hundreds of deer were left to rot before the DNR could shut them down. The DNR recovered an entire pickup truck full of severed trophy heads!

Just the thought of such a waste makes everyone, hunters as well as nonhunters, sick! My heart goes out to the animals. My heart also goes out to Tony and the countless other hunters who painstakingly and legally pursued their quarry only to have their dreams smashed and stolen by such a selfish and senseless act.

Truth be told, my heart breaks the most for the kids and families involved. Don't get me wrong, I'm all in favor of punishments involving the loss of hunting privileges, weapons, and vehicles. I'm also in favor of the heavy fines they will face. These are in my eyes all justifiable. What breaks my heart, though, is that long after the kids have paid for their crimes, people's unforgiveness and bitter hatred toward them will continue.

Proverbs tells us that bitterness is rottenness to the bones! (Proverbs 14:30). People's anger, bitterness, and unforgiveness can often destroy both parties. But they mostly affect the ones who are unwilling to forgive. Unforgiveness rots us from the inside out. When we forgive, as Christ forgave us, it frees us to enjoy and pursue life. When we hold onto that anger, we are letting it have control over our lives. That means the party we are mad at not only hurt us once, but we are also choosing to allow them to continue hurting us.

Matthew 6:14–15 says, "For if you forgive others for their transgressions, your Heavenly Father will also forgive you. But if you do not forgive others, then your Father will not forgive your transgressions."

That's a sobering thought! There are hundreds of people who have never even met these kids who now hate and are embittered toward them. Scripture tells us Be angry, and do not sin; do not let the sun go down on our anger, and do not give the devil an opportunity (Eph. 4:26). Forgive as God has forgiven you. The amazing thing about forgiveness is that it doesn't pardon the crime. It simply frees you from the responsibility of being judge, jury, and executioner. You're simply trusting God to handle the situation as he sees fit, in his perfect time. That's a promise that frees us up to enjoy life, worry free.

Never take your own revenge, beloved, but leave room for the wrath of God, for it is written, "Vengeance is mine, I will repay", says the Lord (Romans 12:19).

We have all screwed up at one time or another, either willfully or unintentionally. Let me share my own run-in with the law.

After several eventful nights in the bear stand, my buddy Scott took off work to film my next bear hunt. Several bears had been hitting my baits, and I was really hoping to get the hunt on film. This was back in the early nineties when hunting shows and videos were still in their infancy.

As we sat perched twenty feet up a huge white pine, all woodland sounds were drowned out by the deafening buzzing of mosquitoes. The first fur bearer on the scene was a big snowshoe rabbit. Thumper was feasting on the Kool-Aid-soaked bread and doughnuts. He was later joined by a plethora of squirrels and birds. I was sure at any moment Bambi and Snow White would come singing into view. Just about everything had made its appearance that night with the exception, of course, of bears.

As the shadows grew darker, the little woodland creatures scattered abruptly as we could hear a bear approaching. He would have to move in quickly if we were going to get him on film. Sadly, minutes passed by until darkness overtook us without him actually making an appearance.

I apologized to Scott. "Sorry, pal, maybe next time. Shooting light is gone, so let's pack it up and move it out."

I snapped my quiver onto my bow and strapped on my fanny pack. Kneeling down, I was tying my bow onto my pull rope when the eerie silence of the bear woods was suddenly broken by a game warden's commands. "Freeze! Don't move!"

After some quick instructions, we climbed down and exchanged some brief pleasantries. He proceeded to check my license and give us the third degree. He then informed us I was getting a ticket for hunting after legal shooting hours.

I was shocked! I honestly never really paid attention to the exact minute I needed to stop hunting before. I would just pack it up when I could no longer see my sight pins. Wisconsin regulates hunting hours to a half hour before sunrise until twenty minutes after sundown. On a cloudy evening, that could mean it's really dark when your time is up. Or if it's clear and you're sitting on a field edge, there could still be fifteen to twenty minutes of good shooting light left, well after legal shooting hours are over.

I was not only shocked but frustrated. I never intended to break the law and quite honestly was unaware that I was. Not only did we miss a day of work, but I also received a hefty fine as well as a criminal record for my crime. I vowed then and there that it would never happen again. I stopped by Walmart the next day and purchased a cheap watch.

I have always tried to obey game laws—yes, even the ones I don't agree with. Ever since that incident many years ago, I have tried to keep an eye on the clock. Like most folks, I hate the thought of big brother watching me. But on the flip side, big brother is the one who put the kibosh on those young poachers.

But what happens when no one is watching you? What if you could get away with it? What would you do with a trophy on the line? I was faced with these questions on more than one occasion. Please allow me to share one with you.

Tony and I were bowhunting elk in north-central Montana. I had drawn an elk tag, but Tony hadn't. With the week drawing to a close, I was left wondering if I would eat yet another tag. We had a few close encounters of the elk kind, but I was offered no shot opportunities.

I was admittedly getting frustrated. I desperately wanted a big bull. It was a lifelong desire and at the very top of my bucket list. I had been blessed with being a part of others' successes, but I confess, I really wanted to close the deal on one myself.

As the week wore on, we decided that some new country might be just the ticket. As Tony's truck rocked and bounced up yet another two track, we carefully studied the BLM map. There was plenty of BLM land available. But the road also passed along some large private parcels.

This private land was owned by a guy with a, let's say, less-than-endearing reputation. It was his land, and those were his elk! If you managed to shoot an elk on BLM land and it crossed his fence, he would not, under any circumstances, let you recover it. Apparently he must have gotten a lot of coal in his stocking as a kid. He was even known to drive the roads in an attempt to herd the elk away from crossing onto public lands.

He was also reputed for prosecuting anyone who dared to trespass. Needless to say, we studied the BLM property lines carefully, so as not to inadvertently cross a property line. Our map study revealed not only property lines but also some intriguing water holes—water holes that were safely located in the center of a large tract of BLM land.

We parked the truck just west of the road that separated the BLM from the private. About thirty yards east of the road was a fence that marked off the private lands.

We hiked off to the west in search of water and lovesick bulls. Mile after mile we searched for the remote water holes, only to come up dry. The deep, steep canyons revealed little in the way of elk sign and no water.

I love exploring new country. You just never know what maybe waiting for you over the next ridge or valley. It may be a buck or bull or possibly just a big shed antler. There is always an adventure awaiting those willing to step out in faith.

That day's adventure was simply in taking in the beautiful scenery. We never saw an animal! The very tough terrain left us exhausted as we hiked back toward the truck. Daylight was fading as we neared our ride home.

Tony said, "Why don't you bugle just for giggles?"

Sure, why not? I moistened the tattered diaphragm hanging from my lips. Putting the old Wayne Carton bugle tube to my mouth, I let out a medium-sized bugle and ended it with a few chuckles. As we listened to my bugle echo down the canyon, I was surprised to hear a response come from the north. Then another bull screamed back from the east.

Tony and I just stared at each other in utter disbelief! "How far?" we both whispered in unison. "Which one is closer?" After a few tense moments, I bugled again, listening intently as they again responded. Both bulls sounded as if they had moved in closer.

With only maybe fifteen minutes of shooting light left, we had to move quickly. The bull in the east sounded a little bit closer, maybe only a 150 yards tops. And surprisingly, it sounded very close to the truck. We made a hasty dash to close the distance. As we trotted past the truck, the bull bugled again from just over the hill.

Now what? Tony dove in behind some trees on the west side of the road while I found some cover on the east side. As Tony called, the bull continued to respond. Sky-lined, the big six-by-six soon crested the hill. As daylight faded, he stopped to destroy an innocent little pine tree a chip shot away.

The bull was broadside and in easy bow range. But ... he stood just on the other side of the fence! What a dilemma! My mind was racing. My dream bull was standing literally less than fifty yards from the truck. I was on public land, but the bull? Well, he was on private land and wouldn't cross the fence.

We were about eight miles from the ranch house—the same ranch house that housed the dirty dog who, just days previously, had driven back and forth in front of my ground blind as he illegally herded the elk away from me. Many would argue that he owed me!

The other bull, also on the other side of the fence, continued to close the distance as darkness soon overwhelmed us. I had dreamed of opportunities like this my entire life. But gratefully, I never did draw my bow. It wasn't for the fear of getting caught that kept me from flinging an arrow that day because I'm sure I could have gotten away with it.

It was me knowing that I would not have accomplished my goal morally. I would have to live with myself. Every time I looked on that big, beautiful rack, I would be reminded of my crime, that I cheated.

Proverbs 15:3 says, "The eyes of the Lord are in every place, Watching the evil and the good."

Romans 14:12 says, "So then each one of us will give an account of himself to God."

My desire is to live my life above reproach. I may not have filled my tag that day, but I did manage to sleep pretty well that night. In no way am I trying to sound holier than thou because I have messed up a lot. But I do desire to not intentionally sin. I have no desire to hurt my Lord and Savior, knowing the cost he paid to forgive me of my sins.

Leave vengeance to the Lord. Walk each day with him as you feel his presence with you. Talk out your situations and temptations with him. That's what friends do. He's your friend, and he's with you and will never forsake you. This is the only way I know of to live your life above reproach, giving no cause for offense. Then, my friends, your sleep will be sweet and you can live with no regrets.

Pleasant dreams!

CHAPTER 28

Perfect Timing

Waiting for the right moment can apply to virtually any situation. Meanwhile, having a lack of patience can get us into a heap of trouble very quickly. When you meet that perfect someone and finally get a date, I would not recommend asking them to marry you that night. Although you may think she's the right one, you will never know because she'll likely change her number and get a restraining order within the hour! Patience is definitely a virtue. Prayerfully considering the right moment is important in life and in hunting.

If we make our move too soon, we will scare them off. If we wait too long, we will miss the moment and they'll be gone from our lives forever. Perfect timing requires a balance between, "You snooze, you lose!" and "Look before you leap!"

Back in 1990, Scott and I took the day off of work to rattle his eighty acres in north-central Wisconsin. We were both super-excited as we chose our first setup. I had become pretty proficient at calling deer, and Scott was eager to see how it all worked. I was feeling pretty confident, having already called in over a dozen bucks in the past week or so. That dozen included an eight-pointer that went on to reside in my freezer.

After arriving at his cabin, we chose some cover along the river for our first ambush site. The little hemlock grove was located just upwind of the river. The river would prevent deer from sneaking around downwind of us. Scott and I were kneeling about thirty yards apart. I was angled southeast while Scott was facing northeast.

Grunt, grunt, stomp! Stomp! My antlers went hard against a small hemlock as I rubbed it vigorously. *Click, click, click, grind, grind!* The antlers were getting quite a workout as my feet kicked the leaves and underbrush. I was doing my best to simulate two bucks fighting.

Minutes later, I could hear deer approaching, first from Scott's direction and then from my own. Then came a lot of crashing, snorting, and brush breaking. The fights were on, and we had ringside seats. There weren't just two bucks fighting but four bucks fighting—two bucks on Scott's side of the grove and two on my side. They were all really ripping it up.

With my tag already filled, all I could do was watch, listen, and wait for Scott to shoot. And wait and wait and wait. Eventually the wind changed and the bucks vacated.

"Why didn't you shoot?" I later asked.

"I never saw them," was his reply. "They were both in bow range, but they stayed directly behind a blowdown."

"Rattling is awesome, ain't it?" I asked.

Scott's normally very stoic German personality was instantly replaced with schoolgirl squeals of excitement! "Let's go try the ridge!" he said.

Our next setup only produced squirrels, but Scott's enthusiasm never waned. "I've got one more place to try before dark," he said.

This time, Scott would be in a ladder stand rather than on the ground. Scott's chosen stand was located just off of a big hemlock and tag alder swamp. I was kneeling in the hardwood leaves about fifty yards up the ridge from him.

I went through my normal rattling sequence again. It didn't take long before we could hear the familiar crunch, crunch, crunch of a deer approaching. Soon a small six-point buck appeared as he cautiously made his way out of the swamp. He was heading directly at me on a heavily used game trail. *Perfect,* I thought. *He'll pass within about ten yards of Scott's stand.*

Twang! Clickety, clank, clank, clank! Scott's aluminum arrow made a terrible racket as it skipped through the trees. The buck spun and headed back off toward the swamp. Stomp, stomp, stomp, snort! I stopped him in his tracks as I stomped the ground and snorted. Then my grunting and bleating turned the buck around as he started back in our direction.

"Cool, now just wait for it, Scott!" I whispered to myself. "If you wait, he'll pass right by."

Twang! Clickety, clank, clank, clank! Another arrow rattled off through the trees. Again the buck spun and retreated toward the safety of the swamp. But again, I stomped, snorted, and stomped again.

I couldn't believe it. He stopped again! As I worked the buck back in with some more grunting and bleating, I kept thinking, *Just let him come in, Scott. Stop launching arrows at thirty and forty yards when he'll pass right by you.*

As the buck cautiously approached for the third time. Twang! The ancient, bear whitetail hunter lobbed yet another arrow through the trees. *Clickety, clank, clank, clank!*

It's a good thing that I was rattling off the ground because I was now rolling around on it, trying everything I could, to not laugh audibly. I quickly tried to regain my composure as I stomped and snorted again. Much to my surprise, he stopped again. But enough was enough! The buck had no idea what that noisy, camouflaged blob in the tree was or why he was throwing stuff at him, but he really wanted no part of it.

This time the little buck circled around Scott, stopping a mere twenty yards from my position. He stayed there, stomping his foot as he did the head bob, trying desperately to identify the still-laughing "stump" in the leaves. The wind finally swirled, giving me away as darkness closed in.

We had an absolutely unforgettable time that afternoon. Scott has since gone on to harvest several nice bucks with his bow. We both learned a lot about timing and patience that day.

In no way do I want to seem as if I'm picking on Scott because I have sure made my share of mistakes over the years. Despite some really odd circumstances, I had one particular hunt go really well a few years back. It happened on my in-laws' farm in southeastern West Virginia.

It was spring turkey season, and I was eager to put a bird down. I had set up on the edge of a hayfield. I was sitting with my back against a mighty oak, and my Excalibur crossbow was resting on my knee. A twenty-acre hayfield was laid out before me. West Virginia is anything but flat, and this rolling field was no exception. It included a deep, steep valley that dropped off just to my left. With my decoys spread out before me, I started to call and wait, only to call and wait some more.

I was about to call it quits after a long, uneventful morning. That's when in the far northwest corner of the field, a nice tom appeared. He was strutting along but never made a peep. He was heading my way but still had about three hundred yards to cover. I sat motionless, yelping occasionally as I let the decoys do most of the work. He eventually disappeared from view into the steep valley below and slightly to my left. I anticipated that when he finally popped out, he would be in bow range.

As I waited for the bird to cover the next hundred yards, I noticed a big black bear appear in the same corner of the field the tom had. The bear waddled into the field and then climbed up the honey tree. The honey tree was a massive old stump about five feet in diameter and about twenty feet tall. The bear climbed to the top of this hollow stump and proceeded to pull a very impressive Pooh bear imitation, eating as much honey as he could before the bees drove him away.

A few minutes passed before the bear shot down the tree and began to roll around in the hay. I would assume he was trying to rid himself of all those angry bees! After a few moments of rolling around, he ran about thirty yards farther into the field before again stopping. Confident he was now rid of the bees, he continued on his merry way, while heading directly at me. After about fifty yards, the bear stopped and stood on his hind legs, staring in my direction. After a few moments, the bear dropped to all fours and began to race across the field right at me.

As if on cue, the tom's red head appeared, coming out of the valley as he zeroed in on my decoys. Fanning out, the big tom began to strut in closer and closer. Time was definitely at a premium, as the tom was sure to notice the charging bear at any moment. The bear disappeared into the valley as the tom worked his way in closer. The tom was only about twenty yards away, but was still too far to my left. If I shot him there, my bolt was sure to sail off down into the valley, never to be seen again. He was also in full strut, which is a shot I personally try to avoid when using archery equipment. The vitals are much harder to identify on a strutting bird.

As the tom moved in closer, I prayed he would come out of strut before the bear spooked him. As if on cue, both the tom and I heard the bear galloping up the hill toward us. With his eyes popping out, the tom immediately came out of strut as the bear suddenly appeared thirty yards away and closing fast. Thwhack! My bolt zipped through the bird. He instantly spun and ran into the woods behind me.

The bear continued running into my decoy setup. He was about twenty yards away and closing when he got a big whiff of this old Tom. Spinning on a dime, he sent dirt flying as he hightailed it for the next county.

Man, I love hunting! What an awesome experience! I trekked back to the house, hoping someone had been watching, while frustrated I had missed the opportunity to get it all on film.

I returned a short time later with my father-in-law and Hailee, my black lab. Hailee quickly found the bird about a hundred yards from where I had shot it. She does her best to retrieve birds but usually just ends up dragging turkeys. After all, a twenty-five-pound tom is a big job for an eighty-pound dog!

I always make every attempt to recover game. Turkeys can often travel quite a distance after being hit with an arrow, often leaving very little in the way of a blood trail. But a good-nosed dog can make pretty quick work of a recovery, even in the thickest of cover.

Later as I sat back and pondered the day's adventures, I was amazed at the timing of it all for me to be in that exact spot, on that precise day and time when a turkey and bear just happened to be there. It was truly incredible! What if that bear popped up a second earlier? What if that tom saw him a second sooner? What if I had waited to shoot for a second longer? What if that bear had taken a few more steps or even decided to climb the tree I was sitting against? He would have literally run right up and over me!

It was late in the morning when that tom first showed himself. I was actually just about to quit when I first saw him. What a missed opportunity that would've been!

There is an appointed time for everything. And there is a time for every event under heaven—

A time to give birth and a time to die;
A time to plant and a time to uproot what is planted.
A time to kill and a time to heal;
A time to tear down and a time to build up.
A time to weep and a time to laugh;
A time to mourn and a time to dance.
A time to throw stones and a time to gather stones;
A time to embrace and a time to shun embracing.
A time to search and a time to give up as lost;
A time to keep and a time to throw away.
A time to tear apart and a time to sew together;
A time to be silent and a time to speak.
A time to love and a time to hate;
A time for war and a time for peace. (Ecclesiastes 3:1–8)

Solomon listed out some real extremes there. But in between the "time to be born and a time to die," we must learn the balance of, a time to shoot and the time to wait for it. Sometimes we jump the gun, like Scott did, and end up with nothing but bent shafts and memories. Other times we give up too soon while our long-awaited breakthrough is on its way, just out of sight in that steep valley.

We learn from experience as we learn to trust the process. We trust the Lord because he has shown himself faithful in the past. We trust him by asking what to do as well as when to do it. After all, they are his perfect plans for our lives. It only makes sense to ask the author of the book what happens next without skipping any pages.

CHAPTER 29

Trust the Process

Mark and I had been hunting hard for weeks, but we didn't have much to show for all our efforts. We had hiked for miles and found a lot of sign but had yet to grasp any bone. Today we would be hunting a familiar sheep farm. This particular farm was one all three of my boys had taken turns working on during their high school years.

Mark was about halfway up the hill in the hardwoods as I paralleled him along the pasture. As I crested a small hill, I froze in my tracks. No, it couldn't be. I slowly brought the binoculars to my eyes and studied its form. If it is, it was huge! My pace intensified as I trotted over to claim my prize.

It was a gorgeous, seventy-inch, four-point shed. Sorry, didn't I mention we were shed hunting? Anyway, the shed antler was absolutely perfect, with a fourteen-inch G2 and no chew marks. I excitedly hollered for Mark.

"We have got to find the other side!" I pleaded excitedly. Within about ten minutes, I found its mate less than a hundred yards away, laying along the fence line. To date, they are my best-matched set.

I absolutely love shed hunting—maybe a little too much if that's even possible. I consider the privilege of walking in the woods and fields for hours each spring to be a real blessing. All a guy really needs to shed hunt is a good pair of boots and a pair of binoculars. The binoculars aren't even necessary, but they can sure save a lot of boot leather as you carefully study things that simply look out of place.

Shed hunting has to be one of the cheapest, healthiest, and most enjoyable sports available. You're basically just taking your dog for a walk in the woods. I have found hundreds of sheds over the years. I can pretty much tell you where, when, and with whom I was with when I found most of them.

Weird? Maybe. But several of these trophies are reminders of some truly wonderful times I spent with my family and friends. Some remind me of a romantic spring walk with my wife. Others remind me of a special laugh or circumstance with one of my sons or friends.

Last year, I managed to find three sheds along fences and ditches as I jogged down country roads. A few years back, I found a small spike moments after I buried our beloved family dog. And how could I possibly forget the sheds I found while taking a few very necessary bathroom breaks. So does a bear go in the woods? You betcha! And apparently, so does Tom!

Some sheds actually remind me of my own human nature. I remember one dry spell when I had looked for about two weeks without finding a thing. Zak and I were about to give up for the day when I spotted a nice set lying in a bed. I ran over and picked up the beautifully matched, double drop-tined pair.

While I admired them, Zak came trudging along down the trail toward me. I felt terrible. The sheds had been lying on the trail he had been walking down, and I had cut him off. I offered them to him, but he declined. He was later rewarded with two of our biggest finds yet.

Often while shed hunting, we come across bucks that didn't quite make it. That particular spring Zak had found two dandies. The first was a massive, wide eleven-pointer that had apparently been hit by a car. The huge buck had crawled under a downed tree in the bottom of a drainage ditch. His head and antlers were frozen tight in the snow and ice, leaving only the tip of one beam and part of a hind leg visible. I'm still amazed Zak spotted him. It took us over an hour to chip out his antlers with our pocket knives.

The following week we were shed hunting at a different farm about twenty miles away. As we canvassed the property, I received a text saying, "Dad, I just found the coolest-looking basket rack!" Apparently we had different ideas as to what a "basket rack" meant.

Zak's basket rack was actually a monster fifteen-pointer with three main beams. I European mounted both of those bucks for Zak. He proudly displayed them in his living room as a reminder of his adventures with Dad. Those two bucks were a constant reminder of what patience and persistence can produce.

Shed hunting is often a feast-or-famine proposition. You can walk for days and even weeks without finding a thing and then drive down the road and spot one lying in a field.

That's exactly what happened to Dave and me a few years back. It was a Saturday morning, and we were going to spend the day shed hunting. I was driving while Dave was enjoying the view. He was looking out over a cut bean field when he hollered, "Sheds!" There, lying side-by-side a hundred yards off the road, was a beautifully matched ten-pointer. With permission to hunt that property, we left with sheds in hand. After five hours of hard hunting, we returned home with only Dave's ten-pointer to show for our efforts.

Shed hunting is a real lesson in patience and persistence. I average a shed every two to three hours of walking. Those are not very good odds. But just knowing they may have dropped late keeps you looking. Every year I manage to find sheds that were dropped the previous year. That means I either walked by them last year or they were shed after I walked through the area. But knowing there can be one just around the next bend keeps me looking and looking hard.

Patience and persistence are necessary virtues for any sportsman. No matter what trips your trigger, you'll be much better off if you learn to trust the process and not to give up.

A few years ago, my wife and I were standing on a fishing dock in Florida, watching the sunset. My attention was soon drawn to the comedy act that was setting up nearby. Two men and a twelve-year-old boy had taken the spot next to us.

While Dad headed back to the truck for a big cooler of beer, "Uncle Billy Bob" coached the chunky youngster in the "ways of the fish." Billy Bob was, without a doubt, the most unique fella I have ever met.

Uncle Billy Bob was a very tall, thin white guy with a very heavy Cajun accent. For reasons only known to him, he was desperately doing his best to convince everyone around him that he was in fact an inner city gangster. He dressed and attempted to talk like one of LA's finest gangster rappers. I cannot do justice in describing the unique verbatim that flowed from his Cajun lips as he tutored Junior in the ways of the fish.

The boys dad had instructed them to cast out their lines and just let the bait sit. Dad returned shortly after Billy Bob told Junior to reel it in, "just to see what it feels like." Dad proceeded to chew them out for their impatience.

"Just trust the process," he said as he cracked open another beer.

Learning to trust the process is one of the hardest things we can do. It's easy to quit when we doubt what we're doing is going to work. But if we focus on our past successes, it is much easier to trust the process. If I look for two weeks without finding a shed, all I have to do is go back and look at the piles of bone I have already found. I'm then reassured that my current drought will not last forever. After all, droughts of differing lengths preceded every antler I ever found.

I have taped inside of my bow case, photos of animals I harvested at the very end of past seasons. When I'm discouraged because of a lack of game or my poor shooting, I look at these photos of my past successes, and they encourage me to hang in there and trust the process as I continue to trust the Lord, while putting in my time.

I have sat across from many angry, heartbroken couples that were contemplating divorce. After hearing them out, I like to encourage them with success stories of the past. I believe there is no broken relationship that is truly beyond hope. But the hurting couple has to buy into the idea and trust the process to actually see positive results.

Likewise, to be a successful hunter, you can't give up before the last minute of the last day. Even if that day comes and goes and you didn't punch your tag, you can start dreaming and planning for next year as you cherish all the good days you had enjoyed.

My first bear season had it all—highs, lows, mosquitoes in sweltering heat, to an early fall snowstorm! I was running two baits about thirty miles north of my house. The west bait produced mixed results with several bears and a game warden frequenting the area.

One night in particular, I checked the trail timer as I baited. It had been set off at four o'clock in the afternoon. Keep in mind this was before the age of trail cameras. Hmmm, four o'clock. That's exactly when Eric baited for me the day before. I reasoned that he must've set it off as he left. Although earlier at work that day, he did share with me that he felt really strange when he was baiting— almost like he was being watched.

After placing the logs on the bait pile and resetting the trail timer, I climbed up the big white pine tree. I strapped in and glanced down to see a big bear at the bait watching me. I hadn't even had a chance to sit down or nock an arrow. The big bear would alternate between looking at me and looking at the bait. He was quartering away when I finally managed to nock an arrow in between his glances.

There was no doubt he knew I was there. After all, he watched me climb up the tree. But like most guys, he was more concerned about eating doughnuts than any possible consequences. Eventually, in between glances, I was able to draw.

I went through my mental checklist and picked a spot right behind his front shoulder. Anchor point? Check! Pick a spot? Check! Squeeze the trigger, thwack! The big bear jumped over the log pile and dove into the thick brushy swamp! He stopped ten yards away and stared back at me! Then he just wandered off.

My shot had gone just where I had aimed but also just where I shouldn't have aimed. The bear was quartering away, and I shot just as he was reaching forward for a doughnut. My arrow flew spot on, harmlessly between his outstretched arm and his chest.

He was the big one—the bear I laid awake dreaming of—and I blew it! I was sick to my stomach. All that work and effort down the tubes. After gathering up some help. We spent the rest of the night on our hands and knees trailing the flesh-wounded bear through the thick underbrush, just to make sure my shot went where I thought it had. I'm certain he recovered and went on to enjoy many more trips to the doughnut shop.

Unbeknownst to us, that big bear had been bedding only five yards behind the bait. The mixture of tall grass, tag alder, young poplars, and berry brush limited our visibility to only a few yards. It's no wonder that we had an uneasy feeling when we baited it. We could have literally spit on him had we known where to spit! Between my miss, the game warden, and a sow with four cubs, I ended up abandoning that bait in lieu of the east bait site.

I had at least two bears hitting the east site—a small, regular attender and a big, occasional attender. I passed on the little guy a few times but never saw the big guy. By the last week or so of season, the action had slowed to a crawl. There was still one bear hitting the bait, but he would circle just out of bow range. Then he would wait until well after dark to commit.

The last day of bear season had finally arrived, and it would be several years before I would be able to draw another bear tag. Since I really wanted a bear, I decided to pack my .30-06 and leave my bow in the truck.

"Let's see you circle out of range now! Come on, bear! Come and say hello to my little friend!"

After shouldering my climbing tree stand and fifty pounds of bear bait, a little voice told me to load up my rifle. It made sense, since it had been raining and the sneak in would be very quiet. I didn't want to waste time loading up completely, since I'd have to unload it again before I climbed into the tree. So I only bothered to put two cartridges in my rifle.

As I snuck around the last bend in the trail, there he was—already chowing down on the bait only twenty yards away! Facing directly away from me, as he inhaled yesterday's offerings. I carefully picked a spot on the black blob and boom! The bear wheeled at the shot and started running down the trail straight at me. I quickly worked the bolt, and boom! I hit him again as he closed the distance.

My gun was now empty, and the rest of my bullets were all tucked safely away in my backpack. Quickly, I spun the gun around, grabbing it by the barrel as I raised the gun above my head like a club. The charging bear then skidded to a stop at my feet.

There he laid, only two steps away was my first bear. Just to be clear, I don't believe the bear was coming after me. I just happened to be standing on the trail, between where he was and where he wanted to be.

I had every reason to give up and not hunt that day. It was a cold, rainy day, and the bears had not cooperated in weeks. Even the law seemed to be against me. But I persisted and hung in there and was blessed with an awesome experience and some delicious meat for the freezer.

Whatever you do you in life, you have to learn to trust the process.

Do you not know? Have you not heard?

The Everlasting God, the Lord, the Creator of the ends of the earth

Does not become weary or tired.

His understanding is inscrutable.

He gives strength to the weary,

And to him who lacks might He increases power.

Though youths grow weary and tired,

And vigorous young men stumble badly,

Yet those who wait for the Lord

Will gain new strength;

They will mount up with wings like eagles,

They will run and not get tired,

They will walk and not become weary. (Isaiah 40:28–31)

The process we need to trust is his plan for your life. His plan is written out in his love letter to you. It's called the Bible. Try giving the New Testament a read today.

For I know the plans that I have for you,' declares the Lord, 'plans for welfare and not for calamity to give you a future and a hope. Then you will call upon Me and come and pray to Me, and I will listen to you. You will seek Me and find Me when you search for Me with all your heart. (Jeremiah 29:11–13)

Jeremiah wrote this promise to the Jews, who had been taken into captivity in Babylon. A teenager named Daniel took those promises to heart and became second-in-command in all the known world, not once but twice in his eighty-plus years of life. He obeyed, believed, and trusted the process!

What are you believing God for today? Patience, my friend! Patience! Trust and obey and watch his promises come true.

CHAPTER 30

The Self Bow

I have been mystified and drawn to the flight of the arrow ever since my ankle-biter days. Bows were always on the top of my holiday wish list. By the time I was twelve, my arrows had whacked an assortment of birds, rabbits, squirrels, snakes, gophers, and chipmunks. But my most remarkable trophy was the woodcock I took in flight with my longbow. I'm the first to confess that luck played a much greater role in that shot than my skills ever did. But I made the shot nonetheless.

My dad originally doubted my amazing feat, assuming I had found the bird, until he examined it and found it to be still warm. Later that year, my paper route money provided me with enough money to purchase my first compound bow, and the rest, as they say, is history.

I have owned many compounds over the years, but I have never lost my love for traditional archery. My longbows and recurves have helped me to stock many freezers over the last forty years. Admittedly, though, my compounds have filled the majority of my tags.

A few years back, I was blessed with a beautiful Osage orange self-bow. A friend of mine had painstakingly handcrafted this gift, along with all its accessories. It came complete with a Flemish bow string, an elk hide grip, mink ball silencers, and a whitetail hair wind indicator. It was absolutely beautiful! The bow also came with a handcrafted leather quiver and a dozen cedar arrows. Six arrows were tipped with broadheads and six with field points. It was an awesome gift, and I could hardly wait to try it out.

Twenty minutes later, I was painfully reminded as to why I used to wear an arm guard and finger tabs. With a swollen, black-and-blue wrist and tender fingers, I sat down to ponder why I couldn't hit squat. My arrows flew everywhere but where they were supposed to. I admittedly had long since lost the strength I needed to shoot my seventy-two-pound longbow.

There was a time when I was quite proficient with my old longbow. I could consistently whack rabbits and squirrels at thirty yards. Nonetheless, I couldn't shoot a decent group with this self-bow at ten yards, let alone thirty. The weeks passed by quickly as I practiced diligently, but I still couldn't hit consistently with the self-bow, and bow season had now arrived.

What should I do? Besides my desire to hunt with it, I didn't want to hurt the feelings of the man who painstakingly made it for me. But it was hunting season, and I didn't trust my shooting with this bow. The risk of wounding an animal wasn't worth it.

Begrudgingly, I knew I had to go back to my training wheels. Yup, I had to blow the dust off my compound and get 'er done! My friends tried to reassure me with comments like, "An arrow is an arrow."

I conceded and told my bowyer friend what I had to do. He was not offended in the least and said he would've done the same thing. He also suggested that it was most likely my arrows that were to blame.

We all set goals in life as well as in our hunting. Some goals maybe no more lofty than harvesting your first deer or possibly your first buck. It usually then escalates to your first Pope and Young animal. Maybe you've even advanced to setting your goals as high as the "elite" Boone and Crockett club. If so, you had better be patient, as those critters are few and far between.

Maybe you're progressing through the weapon goal stages. Most of us start out our hunting carriers using firearms. Then we may advance to the added challenge of archery equipment or possibly even to traditional archery. Traditional archery will definitely grow some hair on your chest. Some dedicated traditionalists will go so far as knapping their own arrowheads.

Personally, I have always wanted to try hunting with a spear. In my eyes, that would have to be the ultimate challenge. That's probably not something this hashtagging generation dreams about, but I sure do! That ultimate level could never be reached sitting on a couch or with a cell phone.

But the common, unifying drive of all hunters is our love of the hunt, matching wits with something much better equipped in the five senses than we are while pursuing them in their living room. The process or methods may vary, but my ultimate goal is to stay in the woods as long as possible. My desire to hunt with that self-bow had gotten me too wrapped up in the method. I had become stressed out over method and lost the joy in the actual process of the hunt.

A few years back, I gave the self-bow another try. But this time, I tried using some aluminum arrows in it. I know there are some traditionalists who are cringing at the thought, but it's hard to argue with success. I was soon shooting accurately out to about fifteen yards with it. That effective range is plenty for whitetails. Game on!

October 20th was a beautiful fall evening. The temperatures were in the sixties, and there was a light south wind blowing in my face. I was sitting in the double ladder stand I mentioned in previous chapters. The golden corn field in front of me was glistening in the afternoon sun. The gorgeous fall leaves surrounding the field were in their peak fall colors! These intense colors combined with the deep blue sky were a virtual assault on my eyes. It was a day when you couldn't help but praise the Lord just to be alive!

My desire that night was to harvest a doe with my self-bow. I had four doe tags burning a hole in my pocket and a large vacancy in my freezer. Shooting a buck really didn't even cross my mind. With the corn still standing, many deer choose to travel the edge of, rather than through, the corn. That meant most of my shots would be limited to less than ten yards, which is well within my effective bow range.

A doe and fawn soon began working their way through the corn from east to west. I slowly stood up and prepared for a shot. The nubby passed by me at about seven yards, between the first and second row of corn. The doe slowly chomped her way along, feeding behind the nubby buck. My fingers tightened on the string as I prepared for the inevitable. She was about twelve yards away when, for reasons only known to her, she turned and started feeding south, deeper into the corn field, eventually disappearing from view.

About a half hour passed before I again heard the telltale sounds of a deer coming through the woods. I turned to my right and was surprised to see a 120-inch eight-pointer. I slowly turned and prepared for a possible shot. The buck was on a collision course with my tree. A few seconds later he stopped, standing broadside at five yards.

Should I? My mind raced as I waffled between self-bow success and the reality of missing out on the entire rut. I had some truly huge bucks on my trail cameras that year, and shooting this buck would eliminate any chance I had to harvest one of them. The whitetail rut was the very thing I looked forward to all year long, and by shooting this buck my season would end before it ever really began.

I chose to let him walk away, totally oblivious as to how close he came to taking a dirt nap. I continued to hunt with my stick bow for another week or so without ever drawing it back.

As the rut heated up, I switched back to my compound for the duration of the season. Truth be told, I never filled my tag that year, but I never regretted my decision either. I love to hunt, and if my season is going to end early, it had better end because I arrowed a real whopper.

I hunted through the rut, as well as throughout December that year. I even battled the subzero temperatures of January. As I sat shivering in my stand on the last day of bow season, my mind drifted back to that warm October afternoon—the one I had that nice eight-pointer at five yards. Did I regret it? Nope, not at all! By not settling on something I really didn't want, I was blessed with an extra eighty hours in the field enjoying God's beautiful creation. I had encounters with an additional forty-six bucks that season, all of which had passed within bow range. Several were bigger than that eight-pointer. But I never had an opportunity at one I really wanted. There is no shame in an empty tag. Nope, I had no regrets at all!

My love for the hunt or for the process of being out there far surpassed my need to be successful in filling a tag. I never want to cut my time outdoors short. This love I have for hunting is similar to our relationship with the Lord. Way too often people can get more wrapped up in the method rather than the process of simply being with their Creator.

Do we love God? Or do we love a religious method? Are we missing out on relationship with the Lord because we are so focused on a particular method or denomination?

We all come from different spiritual backgrounds, and there are a lot of religions out there. But Jesus didn't come to give us another religion, He came to free us from religion and all its trappings. He died to take our sins away and to restore the broken relationship we have with his Father.

Jesus said to him, "I am the way, and the truth, and the life; no one comes to the Father but through Me." (John 14:6)

Do you believe in who Jesus is and what he has done for you? Have you asked him to forgive you and to be your Lord and Savior? That simple prayer restores the lost relationship with the Father. God no longer sees your sin but looks on Jesus's sacrifical blood that is now covering you. His shed blood received by your faith is the only acceptable sacrifice for your sin.

We either belong to God or we don't. We either believe and have received his gift of grace or we have not. We either got the buck or we didn't! There is no catch and release in hunting, and there are no maybes with salvation!

We are hunters. It doesn't matter if you hunt with a bow, gun, or spear—you're a hunter. You either received Jesus as your Savior or you didn't. Religious methods, churches, and processes change, but Jesus Christ is the same yesterday, today, and forever! Jesus never changes, and his love for you never will either.

Why don't you ask him to forgive you and be your Lord and Savior today? I have never regretted it and you won't either!

God bless, and happy hunting!

ABOUT THE AUTHOR

Tom has been an avid bowhunter since he was twelve, and his favorite way to hunt is by calling game. Tom has successfully called in hundreds of whitetails, as well as elk, moose, bears, turkeys, and wolves. He has been happily married to his wife, Darla, since 1986. They have raised three sons and look forward to grandchildren. Tom and Darla currently live in the mountains of West Virginia after spending most of their lives in Wisconsin.

Tom's passion for the outdoors ranks second only to his passion for the Lord. Tom worked as a missionary and pastor for twenty years and now annually shares his experiences at a variety of camps, churches, game feeds, and outdoor shows. If you're interested in having Tom share at your event, please contact him at tom@ScreamingBullMinistries.com or visit his website at www. ScreamingBullMinistries.com.

Anita Schubring is the author's daughter-in-law and did all the illustrations for this book. If you're interested in her work, you can contact her at: anita@ScreamingBullMinistries.com.